Teachings of a Buddhist Monk

Ajahn Sumedho

Teachings of a Buddhist Monk

Ajahn Sumedho

Edited by
Diana St Ruth

Illustrated by
Marcelle Hanselaar

Buddhist Publishing Group
Totnes

Buddhist Publishing Group,
Sharpham Coach Yard, Ashprington,
Totnes, TQ9 7UT. UK
www.buddhismnow.com

ISBN 0-946672-23-7
© Buddhist Publishing Group 2000
© Amaravati Publications 1990
Illustrations © Marcelle Hanselaar 1990

British Cataloguing in Publication Data
Ajahn Sumedho
    Teachings of a Buddhist Monk
    1. Buddhist life
    I. Title II. St. Ruth, Diana
    294.3444
Printed by Lightning Source

In Memory of

Mr & Mrs C. Jackman

Acknowledgements

Grateful thanks to Ajahn Sucitto and to Don Whitbread for looking through the manuscript and offering helpful suggestions.

Contents

Ajahn Sumedho

Robert Jackman (now known as Ajahn Sumedho) was born in Seattle, Washington in 1934. He was brought up in an Anglican family with one elder sister. Between 1951 and 1953, he studied Chinese and history at the University of Washington. Then he served as a medic in the US Navy for four years, and in 1959 he returned to the University to complete his BA degree in Far Eastern Studies.

The studies introduced him to Buddhism through books, while the period of naval service brought him into contact with the Buddhist society of Japan. His desire to help people made him take up a year's service with the US Red Cross as a social worker. After that, in 1961 he undertook a master's degree in South Asian Studies at the University of California, Berkeley, where he graduated in 1963.

He was drawn again to take up service, this time in Sabah, Borneo, where he worked as a teacher in the Peace Corps between 1964 and 1966.

In 1966 he went to Thailand, took up meditation and was ordained as a novice. In May 1967 he received full ordination.

On encountering a disciple of Ajahn Chah, he sought out this meditation master in the forest monastery of Wat Nong Pah Pong. He then became a disciple of Ajahn Chah and remained under his guidance for ten years.

During this period (1967-1977), the now Venerable Sumedho underwent training in several of Ajahn Chah's branch monasteries, and undertook a pilgrimage in India late in 1973. In 1975, Ajahn Chah authorised him to lead a small community of monks in establishing a forest monastery for Western monks.

In 1976, Venerable Sumedho went to visit his parents in America, and during a stop-over in England was invited to stay at a small Buddhist monastery in Hampstead, London. A second visit followed a year later which, though it had not been his intention, was the beginning of his residency in England. Since that time, with much hard work and a lot of good will, two large and impressive establishments have come into being in England: a Forest Monastery in Chithurst, West Sussex, and the Amaravati Buddhist Monastery in Great Gaddesden, Hertfordshire. Venerable Sumedho (the honorific 'Ajahn' means 'teacher' or 'master') presently resides as Abbot at the Amaravati Monastery.

Foreword

I met Ajahn Sumedho in 1967 on a mountain top in Sakolnakorn Province, Northeast Thailand. He was living together with another monk in a cottage in the ruins of an ancient Cambodian mountain temple, after completing his first rains retreat as a fully ordained bhikkhu with Ajahn Chah. There he sat on the corner of the porch of his tiny wooden cottage wearing the dusty robes of a forest monk. The first thing I noticed, after paying respects, was that he was covered with bees. He greeted me and we began talking about the monk's life and the Dharma as if nothing special was happening. Apparently there was a bee's nest at the corner of this cottage and, after his own reflection on this fact, he had simply made his peace with the bees and let them walk all over him. Already I knew I had met a remarkable man. As our conversation about Dharma progressed from my interest in Buddhism to his experiences of practice, my respect for him grew. After a long and lonely first year, sitting as a novice at a temple in Nong Kai Province, he had met a monk from Wat Pah Pong, one of the great forest monasteries, and followed him to meet the teacher, Ajahn Chah. In the forest he had found a way of practice, harder but truer than isolated retreat, and even in a short time I could sense how the integrity and depth of this path of practice had touched him. He said it had not been easy and that Ajahn Chah had not treated him in any special way—which is unusual, since Western monks usually received rather grand treatment in Thailand. He even expressed some doubts about going back again, but the spirit of his words and his connection to the commitment of discipline, honesty and simplicity in the forest life made it sound like he was hooked. I was also hooked by the inspiration of his descriptions. Sometime shortly thereafter I went on the first of many visits to Wat Pah Pong and, after completing my American Peace Corps tenure, I too became a monk with Ajahn Chah.

The climb up to this Cambodian temple at Wat Pupek was, as I recall, about two thousand steps. Ajahn Sumedho tells the story of how in the months following my visit, during the hottest of the hot season in Thailand, he got very sick. He had dysentery and fevers and god knows what other tropical ailments, and became far too weak to walk down the mountain several miles to a nearby village and then up the mountain again simply to collect his day's food. Instead he lay sick, stuck on the wooden floor of a small hut at the foot of the mountain several miles from the next village. This hut, as many in Thailand, had a corrugated tin roof which made it function as a particularly fine oven under the punishing rays of the hot-season sun. I visited him also in this hut and he told me that his weakness and fevers had made it so impossible for him to collect alms food that devoted villagers from the nearby villages were coming and dropping off food for him so that he might eat each day. As he describes it, he lay there sick, feverish, isolated, roasting hot and miserably unhappy. All of the doubts that could and do assail a young monk or beginning meditator took over his mind.

Why was he doing this to himself, anyway, living in such a wretched condition in these strange Buddhist robes—for what purpose, to what benefit? He questioned for himself: 'Why did I ever ordain, why did I start meditating?' Why did he not simply disrobe and return to the West to enjoy good health, easy living, music, camaraderie of friends, and a full and happy life? The sicker and hotter he got, the stronger became the doubts. He says these doubts more than doubled his misery. The heat and the sickness of the body were bad enough, but having the mind filled with doubts, with resentment, agitation and confusion, was much worse. Somehow, looking at himself in the height of his misery, he saw and understood that it was HE who was creating most of the suffering he was experiencing at that moment. It was he who was creating the suffering of doubting, restlessness, agitation and confusion. And then he simply decided to commit himself to the monk's life and end the suffering of doubting, restlessness and confusion. He let go of the suffering of his mind and accepted his situation as a monk, even in these difficulties, and has not turned back for the nearly twenty-five years that have followed.

It is just the qualities of strength, straightforwardness and perseverance illustrated in this story that Ajahn Sumedho has brought to his practice and his teachings. He urges us to live with things as they are, directly, simply and mindfully. He teaches the freedom of having no preferences, and he has amply demonstrated the wisdom of this way of life over and over again in the difficulties of his own training and teaching as a monk.

As did the Buddha and Ajahn Chah, Ajahn Sumedho teaches suffering and its end. In the first year-long retreat he did as a novice, alone in a hut in Nong Kai Province, he had faithfully practised the art of meditation. In these long months of solitary intensive practice, he experienced many of the traditional insights and samadhi states that are the fruit of such retreats. But then, under his teacher, Ajahn Chah, he discovered a wisdom beyond all states and all conditions, a spirit of the Dharma of attaining nothing. His practice and teaching became focused on just what is here and now in this moment. Whatever arises in this moment is the place of our suffering and bondage and is the place of our liberation.

All his teaching points to an immediate mindfulness of this very body and mind. It is not through philosophy or special practices, but here, that wisdom arises, Ajahn Sumedho has brought the simplicity of the forest life and the freedom of the Dharma that grasps at nothing, and offered it to students in the West. To live the holy life, the life of freedom, is to stand nowhere, to possess nothing, to take no fixed position, to open to what is, moment after moment.

This freedom is in him. As a teacher, he brings a spontaneity, wonderful humour and warmth, a terrible, self-revealing honesty, and a clear and uncompromising wisdom. In his years of practice and teaching, he describes wrestling with his own loneliness and weakness, with his anger, fear and pride and, in doing so, invites us all to look most honestly at our own hearts and minds.

In many ways, Ajahn Sumedho has become the most successful abbot of any Western Buddhist monastery and a cornerstone in the development of the ordained Sangha in the West. He teaches the monk's life without a spirit of grasping or rigidity. Instead he brings to this ancient form a tremendous sense of joy and freedom. He loves the monastic life and so people gather around him to enjoy his joy and love and to let the practices of the Dharma that have transformed him transform them as well. Often the monk's life has been used as a vehicle to attain meditative states, jhanas, psychic powers, stream entry, and more. But for Ajahn Sumedho (and for the Buddha as well), the holy life of the monks and nuns is not just a vehicle to be used to grasp after or attain something. It is actually an expression of enlightenment. The joy and simplicity, the letting go into its forms, are what Ajahn Sumedho invites his ordained followers to participate in. He invites them to use the form as a means of coming home to themselves, of making peace with what is.

Spiritual life is not about becoming someone special but discovering a greatness of heart within us and every being. It is an invitation to inwardly drop our opinions, our views, our ideas, our thoughts, our whole sense of time and ourselves, and come to rest in no fixed position. Ajahn Sumedho invites us all, ordained and lay people alike, to enjoy the freedom beyond all conditions, a freedom from fears, from gain and loss, from pleasure and pain. This is the joy and happiness of the Buddha.

Perhaps this is too exalted a description of his way of practice. I dare not praise him too much—he would just make fun of it. Yet so many of us who know him feel blessed, delighted, instructed, and profoundly fortunate to have Ajahn Sumedho in our lives. This book that follows is one small part of the wealth of Dharma that Ajahn Sumedho has brought and offered to the West.

Jack Kornfield
Spirit Rock Center
California, March 1990

Teachings of a
Buddhist Monk

Let go of Fire

The Buddha's teaching is all about understanding suffering—its origin, its cessation, and the path to its cessation. When we contemplate suffering, we find we are contemplating desire, because desire and suffering are the same thing.

Desire can be compared to fire. If we grasp fire, what happens? Does it lead to happiness? If we say: 'Oh, look at that beautiful fire! Look at the beautiful colours! I love red and orange; they're my favourite colours,' and then grasp it, we would find a certain amount of suffering entering the body. And then if we were to contemplate the cause of that suffering we would discover it was the result of having grasped that fire. On that information, we would, hopefully, then let the fire go. Once we let fire go, then we know that it is something not to be attached to. This does not mean we have to hate it, or put it out. We can enjoy fire, can't we? It is nice having a fire, it keeps the room warm, but we do not have to burn ourselves in it.

When we really contemplate suffering, we no longer incline towards grasping hold of desire, because it hurts, is painful, there is no point in doing it. So, from that time on, we understand, 'Oh! That's why I'm suffering; that's its origin. Ah! *now* I understand. It's that grasping hold of desire that causes me all this misery and suffering, all this fear, worry, expectation, despair, hatred, greed, delusion. All the problems of life come from grasping and clinging to the fire of desire.

The human habit of clinging to desire is ingrained. We in the West think of ourselves as sophisticated and educated, but when we really begin to see what is going on in our minds, it is rather frightening—most of us are horribly ignorant. We do not have an inkling of who we are, or what the cause of suffering is, or of how to live rightly—not an inkling. Many people want to take drugs, drink, and do all kinds of things to escape suffering—but their suffering increases.

How conceited and arrogant we Western people can be, thinking of ourselves as civilised! We are educated, it is true, we can read and write, and we have wonderful machines and inventions. In comparison the tribal peoples in Africa, for example, seem primitive, superstitious, don't they? But we are all in exactly the same boat! It is just that *our* superstitions are different. We actually believe in all kinds of things.

For instance, we try to explain our universe through concepts, thinking that concepts are reality. We believe in reason, in logic—which is to say we believe in things we do not know. We have not *really* understood how it all begins and ends. If we read a book and believe what it tells us, believe what the scientists say, we are just believing. We think: 'We're sophisticated. We believe in what the scientists say. People have PhDs—we believe in what *they* say. We don't believe in what witch-doctors say; they're stupid and ignorant.' But it is all belief, isn't it? We still do not know—it just sounds good. The Buddha said we should find out for ourselves and then we do not have to believe others.

We contemplate the universe as impermanent; we can see the impermanent nature of all conditions. From this contemplation, wisdom arises. There is nothing we can find in changing conditions that has any kind of self-continuity. All things begin and end; they arise out of the void and they go back into the void. And wherever we look we are not going to find any kind of permanent personality, or self. The only reason we think we have a personality is because we have memories, ideas and opinions about ourselves. If we are intellectual, we are always up in the head, thinking about everything. Emotionally we might not be developed at all—throw temper tantrums, scream and yell when we do not get our own way. We can talk about Sophocles and Aristotle, have magnificent discussions about the great German philosophers and about Ramakrishna, Aurobindo, and Buddha, and then somebody does not give us what we want and we throw a tantrum! It is all up in the head; there is no emotional stability.

There was a monk I knew once who was quite sophisticated compared to some of the other monks. He had lived in Bangkok for many years, been in the Thai navy, could speak pidgin English. He was quite intelligent and rather impressive. But he had this terrible health problem and felt he could no longer exist on one meal a day. In fact his health was so bad that he had to disrobe [leave the Buddhist Order]. After that he became an alcoholic! He could give brilliant talks whilst being smashed out of his mind. He had the intellect, but no morality or concentration.

On the other hand, we can have very strict morality and not have any wisdom. Then we are moral snobs, or bigots. Or we can become attached to concentration and not have any wisdom. 'I'm on a meditation retreat and I've developed some concentration, some insight, but when I go home, oorh! I don't know if I'll be able to practise any more, or even if I'll have time. I have so many duties, so many responsibilities.' But how we live our ordinary lives is the real practice. Retreats are opportunities for getting away from all those responsibilities and things that press in on us, so as to be able to get a better perspective on them. But if the retreats are just used to escape for a few days and that is all, then they are of no great value. If, on the other hand, they are used for investigating suffering—'Why do I suffer? Why am I confused? Why do I have problems? Why is the world as it is?'—then we shall find out if there is anything we can do about suffering. We shall find that out by investigating this body and this mind.

Ignorance is only the scum on the surface, it does not go deep; there is no vast amount of ignorance to break through. That ignorance here and now, that attachment to the fire here and now—we can let it go. There is no need to attach to fire any more—that is all there is to it. It is not a question of putting out the fire. But if we grasp it, we should let it go. Once we have let the fire go, then we should not grasp it again.

In our daily lives, we should be mindful. What does it mean to be mindful? It means to be fully aware right here, concentrating on what is going on inside. We are looking at something, for instance, and we try to concentrate on that; then a sound comes, and then a smell, then this and then that—distractions, changes. We say: 'I can't be mindful in this environment; it's too confusing. I have to have a special environment where there are no distractions, then I can be mindful. If I go to one of those retreats, then I can be mindful; no distractions there—peace and quiet—noble silence! I can't be mindful in Edinburgh or London—too many distractions. And I've got family, children, too much noise!'

But mindfulness is not necessarily concentrating on an object. Being aware of confusion is also being mindful. If we have all kinds of things coming at our senses—noises, people demanding this and that—we cannot concentrate on any one of them for very long. But we can be aware of the confusion, or the excitement, or the impingement; we can be aware of the reactions in our own minds. That is what we call being mindful. We can be mindful of confusion and chaos. And we can be mindful of peace and tranquillity.

The path of mindfulness is the path of no preferences. When we prefer one thing to another, then we concentrate on it: 'I prefer peace to chaos.' So, then, in order to have peace, what do we do? We have to go to some place where there is no confusion, become a hermit, go up to the Orkneys, find a cave. I found a super cave once off the coast of Thailand. It was on a beautiful little island in the Gulf of Siam. And it was my sixth year as a monk. All these Westerners were coming to Wat Pah Pong—Western monks. And they were causing me a lot of sorrow and despair. I thought: 'I don't want to teach these people; they're too much of a problem; they're too demanding; I want to get as far away from Western monks as possible.' The previous year I had spent a Rains Retreat[1] with five others. Oh, what a miserable Rains Retreat that was! I thought: 'I'm not going to put up with that! I didn't come here to do that; I came here to have peace.' So I made some excuse to go to Bangkok and from there I found this island. I thought it was perfect. They had caves on the island and little huts on the beaches. It was the perfect set-up for a monk. One could go and get one of those huts and live in it. And then go on alms-round in the village. The village people were all very friendly, especially to Western monks because to be a Western monk was very unusual.

---

[1] A time when a monk remains in his monastery for meditation.

We could depend on having all the food we could possibly eat, and more. It was not a place that was easy to get to, being out in the Gulf of Thailand, and I thought: 'Oh, they'll never find me out here, those Western monks; they'll not find me here.' And then I found a cave, one with a *jongrom*,[2] and it was beautiful. It had an inner chamber that was completely dark and no sounds could penetrate. I crawled in through a hole and inside there was nothing. I could neither see nor hear anything. So it was ideal for sensory deprivation: 'Oh, this is exactly what I've been looking for; I can practise all these high *jhanic* states. I can go in this cavern and just practise for hours on end with no kind of sense stimulation.' I really wanted to see what would happen. But there was this old monk living in this cave who was not sure whether he was going to stay. Anyway, he said I could have the grass hut on the top of the hill. I went up there and looked, and down below was the sea. I thought, 'Oh, this is also nice because now I can concentrate on the sea, which is tranquillising.'

There was a Thai monk on the island who was

---

[2] A path for walking meditation.

a very good friend of mine and he said: 'Well, if they find you here, there's an island about fifteen miles further out—they'll never find you there. There's a little hut there, and a little village; the people in the village would love to take care of a monk.' So I was thinking: 'You know, possibly after the Rains Retreat, I will go out to that further island.'

I really was determined to escape. I wanted peace and I found the Western monks very confusing. They would always ask lots of questions and were so demanding. So I was all set to spend the Rains Retreat in this idyllic situation. And then—this foot! My right foot became severely infected and they had to take me off the island into the local hospital on the mainland. I was very ill. They would not let me go back to the island and I had to spend the Rains Retreat in a monastery near the town. Sorrow, despair and resentment arose towards this foot—all because I was attached to tranquillity. I wanted to escape the confusion of the world; I really longed to lock myself in a tomb where my senses would not be stimulated, where no demands would be made on me, where I would

be left alone, incognito, invisible. But after that I contemplated my attitude; I contemplated my greed for peace. And I did not seek tranquillity any more.

I never did return to that island. The foot healed fairly well and I had a chance to go to India. Then, after that I went back to Wat Pah Pong, and by that time I had decided not to make preferences. My practice would be 'the way of no preferences'; I would just take things as they came. On my return to Wat Pah Pong I was put in the responsible position of being a translator for Ajahn Chah. I detested having to translate for Westerners, but there I was. I had to do it, and I also had to teach and train monks. A year or so after that they even sent me off to start my own monastery! Within two years there were about twenty Western monks living with me. Then I was invited to England.

And so I have never escaped to that cave because I no longer made preferences. The responsibilities and teaching seem to be increasing, but it is part of the practice of 'no preferences'. And I find, through this practice, my mind is calm and peaceful. I no longer resent the demands made on

me, or dwell in aversion or confusion about the
never-ending problems and misunderstandings that
arise in human society. So the practice is—just
mindfulness. No longer do I long for tranquillity.
Tranquillity comes and I see it as impermanent.
Confusion comes—impermanent; peacefulness—
impermanent; war—impermanent. I just keep seeing the impermanent nature of all conditions and I
have never felt more at peace with the world than
I do now, living in Britain—much more so than
I ever did when I was, say, those few days on
that island. At that time I was clinging desperately
to ideals of what I wanted and there was the
accompanying fear of having them taken away—I
was afraid that Westerners would come and bother
me and that my peaceful environment would
be interfered with. There was a real selfishness
involved in that rejection and shutting out of
others, and a real fear that others might ruin it for
me. So this attachment to peace and conditions
inevitably brings fear and worry along with it,
because all conditions can easily be taken away
or destroyed. The kind of peace that we can get
from 'no preferences', however, can never be taken

away. It can never be taken away because we can adapt; we are not dependent upon the environment for tranquillity; we have no need to seek tranquillity, or long for it, or resent confusion. So, when we reflect on the Buddha's teaching (seeing suffering, its origin, its cessation and the path to its cessation), we can see that he was teaching the path of 'no preferences'.

The Buddha was enlightened. He spent six years as an ascetic, doing tranquillising practices, attaining the highest states of absorption, and he said: 'No! This isn't it! This is still suffering. This is still delusion.' And, from that realisation he found the Middle Way, the path of 'no preferences', the path of awareness.

We should not expect high degrees of tranquillity if we are living in an environment where people are confused or not tranquil, or where we have a lot of responsibilities and duties. We should not think: 'Oh! I want to be somewhere else; I don't want to be here.' Then we are making a preference. We should observe the kind of life that we have, whether we like it or not—it is changing, anyway; it does not matter.

In life 'like' tends to change into 'dislike'; 'dislike' tends to change into 'like'. Even pleasant conditions change into unpleasant ones, and unpleasant conditions eventually become pleasant. We should just keep this awareness of impermanence and be at peace with the way things are, not demanding that they be otherwise. The people we live with, the places we live in, the society we are a part of—we should just be at peace with everything. But most of all we should be at peace with ourselves—that is the big lesson to learn in life. It is really hard to be at peace with oneself. I find that most people have a lot of self-aversion. It is much better to be at peace with our own bodies and minds than anything else, and not demand that they be perfect, that we be perfect, or that everything be good. We can be at peace with the good and the bad.

Tools to Use

There are two basic practices of Buddhist meditation. The first one is the way of developing concentration and tranquillising the mind. And the second one is the way of developing insight.

Through watching the breath, the mind clears and one becomes absorbed into the sensation of breathing. Then the mind is tranquil and clear. This is the first practice and is a very good thing to develop. Initially, of course, we may find it difficult, or we may even find we have an aversion towards it, but through practice we can become skilful.

The second practice, insight meditation, is simple, but those of us who are impatient do not always find it so. We may have ideas of what should be happening and try to *make* it happen; we may get deluded by our doubts, not knowing what to do next; we may feel bored and restless; we may get caught in changing phenomena. If we find ourselves getting caught in this way, we should stop, detach from it, observe and investigate. Great feelings are sometimes very hard to detach from—so much energy aroused—and the body has a strong reaction. So we should observe the body.

What does the body feel like—the sensations in the heart, in the stomach, in the abdomen? We should bring our attention to the body itself, reflecting on its nature. The body is changing; it was born and it will die. This is the characteristic of all phenomena, mental or physical. Thought, memory, consciousness, all have the same characteristic of beginning and ending, being born and dying. The body is the coarsest thing we have; it seems to be our most solid and permanent possession. Thoughts—they are always changing. And sound—can you keep a sound? Is there such a thing as a permanent sound, or a permanent odour that we can say is really ours? Pain, physical pain sometimes seems like an eternity, but it is not. Pleasure, of course, goes much too quickly; we would like it to stay longer. Fear, worry, remorse, guilt, mental dullness, torpor, sleepiness, happiness—all these things change. No permanency is to be found in any of them. The body, seemingly, is the most stable of them all. But it too changes.

Any form of suffering has a feeling of eternity about it; anything that is painful—despair, anguish, sorrow—these all seem as though they will go on forever. But 'forever' is impermanent, it is a concept. An hour of pleasure is like five minutes. Five minutes of pain is like an hour. Time is relative. We think of time as twenty four hours a day, three hundred and sixty-five days a year, something objective and scientific, but mentally it is a very emotional kind of thing.

There is that which is beautiful, lovely to the eye, to the ear, beautiful fragrances, tastes, pleasurable sensations to the body, beautiful thoughts—fascinating, romantic, lovely, altruistic. Then there is the reverse of all that—the ugly, the unharmonious, the stinking, the unpleasant, pain, hunger, thirst, unpleasant thoughts and memories. We should observe these, note their nature, note their characteristics—whether pleasant or unpleasant, lovely or hideous. Whatever they are like, they all have the characteristic of change, impermanency. Unless we are terribly wise to begin with, we really do not notice this. The Buddha pointed it out to his disciples: 'Look and see for yourselves. Can you find anything permanent? Investigate! Look into things. Be the one who observes, who is aware. Don't be the blind one, the one who just follows his habits,' winds up like a mechanical toy and then runs down.

As human beings we have the ability to reflect. We do not have to be mechanical; there is no need for us to be victims of habit. But we shall be if we do not bring awareness to our lives, if we do not investigate, enquire, look directly into the present moment: 'Who am I? Why was I born?' These are the unanswerable questions we ask ourselves. 'What happens when I die?' Human beings can ask these questions, can reflect and can observe. Wisdom is within each one of us; it is not something that is far away, or something that we have to get hold of or accumulate. There is not one of us lacking in perfect wisdom.

As human beings we have the misfortune of

habitually identifying with changing phenomena as 'me' or 'mine': 'This body is *me*, it's *my* body.' And we spend a lot of time identifying with it and trying to preserve it. Somebody insults it, we feel offended. Somebody praises it, we feel happy. Somebody hits it, we get angry: 'They're hitting me!' Somebody we like gives us a loving pat, we feel happy and joyful: 'They love me! They love my body.' We cling to this coarse body as 'ours': 'I am a man;' 'I am a woman;' 'I am beautiful;' 'I am young;' 'I am old and ugly;' or whatever. However it may appear to us, we consider it to be ours.

The price we pay for identifying with this body in this way is that we suffer. Even though we might have the illusion of being young, beautiful, intelligent—eventually it all changes. No matter how much we do not want the body to age and get sick and die, it does it anyway. So can we really say: 'It's my body; this is me'?

We should look at this body, investigate it: 'What is it?' Ajahn Chah would say that the body is just a place you are temporarily renting: 'It doesn't belong to you, so don't get upset about what happens to it. Take proper care of it; don't mistreat it; feed it properly. But don't regard it as your possession. Don't get infatuated or attached to it. Because if you do, you'll suffer.'

This also applies to our emotions, thoughts and memories: 'Ten years ago . . . ;' 'Fifteen years ago . . . ;' 'Five years ago . . .' our personal history. We identify with it. We have diaries and pictures, photographs taken of when we were babies and when we were in school. We like to look and think: 'I looked like that ten years ago. That was me.' We feel safe and warm when we think that we existed in the past. But what are memories? Can we keep a memory for any length of time? Does it come and go? Does it have any solid substance to it? Is it a reality? What is it? And what is thought? If we think a very high thought: 'Save all the suffering beings in the world!', or a low, mean one: 'Exploit! Hurt! Be cruel to all the living beings in the world!' what these two kinds of thought have in common is that they are only thought. They begin and they end—both of them. One gives pleasure; one gives pain. One is beautiful; one is ugly. But beauty and ugliness, pleasure and pain, high thinking and low thinking all have the same characteristic of impermanence. So we keep reflecting, investigating, noticing, being aware. Sensations in the body, physical pain—we can look at these as well. There is no need for us to habitually react to these things by running away. We can look at pain, and at pleasure. What do we feel like when we are upset? What is it like when we are depressed? We can look at what it does to our bodies, and we can learn.

These thoughts, emotions and sensations are our teachers, and through the practice of awareness, we shall be allowing wisdom to function. We shall not find 'the wise one', we shall never be able to *find* wisdom, but we shall be wise. Wisdom is something we *are* already. Being wise means being aware; it does not mean indulging in emotions and moods; it means being aware of them as they come and go, allowing them to be as they are, not trying to analyse them, or figure them out, saying: 'What does this fascinating sign mean?'

Some people get fascinating signs in their practice. They see lights or have strange visions, and they immediately get fascinated by them, thinking: 'This is a special sign; I'm a special person!' It is all just mad memories, mad perceptions.

The Zen Buddhists have a saying: 'If you see the Buddha, kill him!' So, some people have these mad perceptions: the Buddha comes down and says: 'Listen, friend, you're enlightened. I'm the Buddha and I'm saying this to you.' This has happened, but such things are nothing but creations. We can create anything we want—Jesus Christ, Buddha, Mohammed, Krishna. I met a man in India once, an Englishman, who thought he was Lord Krishna.

We are not trying to become Krishna or Buddha; we are not trying to conceive things and then make ourselves into images of those things, or model ourselves into forms again—that is more birth and death. We may be Lord Krishna for awhile, but then we die again. It does not really matter if we are Lord Krishna or Buddha, or Jim, or Jane. They all have the same characteristic of impermanency. So let us not get fascinated with exotic names and concepts. They are all the same, and just the same as the mundane ones. Jim, Jane, Buddha,

Krishna—they are only concepts and names, conventions.

So being the wise one is being the one who knows. We can be wise right now. We never *become* wise; we never *attain* wisdom. How can we attain what we have already? We just start using it, that is all. And we use it by bringing awareness to our lives, reflecting on our bodies and on our mental conditions, on our moods, feelings, emotions, physical sensations, and on our consciousness through the senses—through the ear, eye, nose, tongue, and body.

The body and mind that we have, that we are renting temporarily, is our teacher. It is teaching us about the nature of all compounded phenomena. This is a lesson we have to learn. And we can learn it in this lifetime. If we do learn it, we shall not have to go through all of this again. If we do not learn it, we *shall* have to go through it again, some other time. So, people who have the good fortune to be bored with the whole process already, if they are bored with being attached to changing things, identifying with all the pieces, the fragments that are experienced through the senses, bored with clinging possessively to things of no value, bubbles . . . , if they are bored with doing those things, then they are Buddhists. And to be a Buddhist means to be wise, to live with awareness, mindfully, reflecting on what is present.

These two practices—concentration and insight—are tools that we can use. We can use them in a formal way, but we can also use them when we are walking, working, standing still, or lying down. We can learn to interfere with our habits, mental and physical. There is no point in just blindly indulging in our emotions, in attraction or aversion; we should *STOP!* We should learn to interfere, learn to look into, learn to confront. Everything in us is being pulled outward through our senses. We look at something beautiful—a beautiful car, a beautiful house—and we want it. This is the desire to grasp, to identify with, to possess. This is what desire does; it pulls us outward all the time. When we just follow desire, we are always identifying with the objects of our senses, grasping at them, or rejecting them. That which is ugly or unpleasant to the senses is rejected, destroyed or repressed. This is the way nature works. If we identify with desire then we are always going to be enslaved by it. It will always pull us this way and that, drive us absolutely mad! There is no end to desire, it just goes on and on and on. Is there any way to completely gratify a desire? If we satiate ourselves—if, for example we eat so much that we stuff ourselves full of food—then suddenly we have no more desire for food, we have an aversion to it. But before long the desire is there again and so we eat more, and then we do not want any more . . . And we keep going on like that—gratifying desire without understanding it.

Sometimes meditators think they should not have desires or should not have greed or lust, or they think they should not like beautiful things, or should not be this way or that way. But these are more concepts. Thinking we should *not* be, we should *not* have, we should not be the way we are—the moods, the faults, or whatever—this is wrong view. Things are just as they are. The body is as it is. Thoughts come and go according to conditions. Good thoughts, bad thoughts, fine ones, mean ones, whatever—they are a part of nature, all of them. But none of them belongs to us. These things are conditions that arise and pass away, they are born and they die from moment to moment.

Through awareness we no longer identify and attach to such thoughts—this is liberation into immortality. And this we cannot conceive. Can we conceive of anything that does not begin and end? What is the beginning of immortality? What is the end of it? We can philosophise about it till doomsday—it will not help at all. So we bring our practice down to practical living, right now in the present moment, to awareness in the present moment, from one moment to the next. It's through resolute, constant awareness that we develop

One Inhalation

The mental world is so powerful and strong, and our minds get so confused, that we get carried away by emotions or by the appearance of things. We really need to establish a point that we can use for meditation, such as our breathing. We are always breathing wherever we are, whether in a quiet place, or in Piccadilly Circus. So, even if we cannot stay anywhere for very long, at least we can stop the mind wandering and being pulled into everything going on around us. We may not get really good concentration in a place like Piccadilly Circus, but at least we can stop ourselves from being attracted to or repelled by extreme sensory impingements. We can bring our attention to the inhalation and the exhalation of the breath.

Some people assume that the purpose of mindfulness of breathing is in order to get high levels of concentration. We should note, however, that the assumptions we make about this practice are just assumptions. The practice itself is as it is; it is for nobody; it is for its own reward—as it is. When we are with the breath, our minds are not thinking about other things, so we are just with the breath. And if we keep with the breath, then our minds will calm down. Breathing, just ordinary breathing, is a calming kind of rhythm; it tranquillises. So mindfulness of breathing is, in itself, its own reward.

We may not realise that each moment with the breath is a tranquil one and so tend to get caught up in trying to acquire something, in trying to get more from it than it can offer us. So we miss the actual result as it is happening. This is human ignorance. We expect something, so we are unaware of what really happens. Now, if we just contemplate what an inhalation is like, we shall see it is not exciting, thrilling, interesting, or fascinating; but neither is it painful, repulsive, or unpleasant. We shall probably consider it to be boring, because we tend to demand a high level of interest and excitement from everything in life. We tend to regard something that is neutral to be boring. But it is not really boring. If something is interesting, it means it holds our attention. If we are reading a book and it interests us, we just sit there; we can hardly tear ourselves away. We do not want to answer the telephone; we do not want to talk to anybody; we just want to remain absorbed in that fascinating, interesting book. If we are reading a boring book, on the other hand, then we shall use every excuse there is to get away from it. The telephone rings; we gladly get up and answer it. The milkman comes; we run to the door, try to chat to him for a bit. If it is boring, there is nothing to hold our attention, so our attention will go to anything, even to things more boring than the book—to get away from one boring thing, we go to another boring thing.

So we try to make life interesting—interesting friends, interesting things to think about, interesting things to do. I am not criticising, I am just pointing out that we spend much of our lives in search of interest. And when something is no longer interesting, then we tend to reject it. If a friend is going through a bad time, say, and he is pretty boring and uninteresting, we tend not to want to be bothered with him. When he is fascinating and scintillating, we enjoy his company because it keeps us interested. But then when he gets boring again, we just want to get away!

Mindfulness of breathing is not interesting and we do not need to make it such. An inhalation is just that, an inhalation. If we say it is interesting or boring, these are judgements we make according to our moods. But in itself, it is just suchness, it is just the way it is. When we reflect in this way, then an inhalation is just that way, and an exhalation is just that way. And when we are not demanding that they be otherwise or looking for something more than is there, then our attitudes are developing in the right direction. So we can use just this one thing, this one practice of mindfulness of breathing, for concentration, for reflection, for understanding, for understanding the way things really are, for understanding why the world is the way it is.

Why *is* the world the way it is? Why is there so much contention, divisiveness, quarrelling and ingratitude? Everything is divided into groups, factions, individuals, each demanding all kinds of things from themselves and from others. We get confusion and depression when people's minds operate on that level. It is winter, the snow is on the ground, and here at Amaravati we have certain emergency situations when the water mains burst. But that is not what happens all the time, is it? Even though yesterday I began to think it was! Sitting here, it is just the way it is. Most of our lives are not incredibly exciting or interesting, they are just ordinary, just the way they are—walking from here to the dormitories, sitting in meditation, getting up, lighting incense sticks, going to the loo, doing some work, eating the meal and so forth. The day goes on like that. Whether we like it or not depends on whether we are inspired, or expecting a lot, or whether we are fed up. If we are fed up, then we can make a big scene. Washing dishes, for example—if we are inspired and really want to work for the welfare of the community, then we go at the dishes with all the energy that comes from love and inspiration. But when we are fed up and do not care any more, then the rota comes up and we do the dishes—we do it, but with no love at all—get there late, break a dish, do not clean up very well. But actually washing dishes is just as it is, isn't it? There is nothing overly pleasant or unpleasant about it; it is just the way washing dishes is. Beyond that we can make anything out of it. Whether we love or hate to do the dishes is something we create, something we superimpose, onto the actual event. The same with an inhalation or an exhalation—it is just that way.

If we try to get high by thinking: 'I'm going to wash these dishes because of my great love for the monks, nuns, and community, and because this is the greatest place in the world,' then inevitably we shall go to the other extreme. But when we can just move towards the way it happens to be—washing dishes, cleaning the room, walking from here to the dormitory, sitting in meditation and watching the breath—that is all right. And then the extreme situations like a water main bursting is also just the way it is. But if we are not expecting any interference in our lives, and we are sitting there, and then someone comes up and says: 'The water main's burst.' I think: 'Damn it! The water main's burst. They're interfering with my meditation. This is a meditation retreat and the water main's burst and it's interfering with my tranquillity!' Then I am feeling that water mains should somehow only burst when I am not on retreat! When they do burst, therefore, it is frustrating; it seems like a kind of plot against me, to give me a bad time. Actually, of course, whether the water main bursts when I am on a retreat or not is still just the way it is. We can always have a place for whatever happens, because it is never something that should not happen.

Through wise reflection, we need not suffer from any turn of events. If we adapt wisely to situations in life, then we do not create the conditions for unnecessary misery. There is always going to be a certain amount of natural suffering, of course, from having been born as a human being. Birth, growing up, sickness, old age and death—these are the results of having been born as a human being. The body, the seasons of the year—such things cannot satisfy us. When we contemplate them and meditate on them, however, then we can be at peace with them.

But then there is also the suffering which *we*

create. If I am sitting here thinking: 'Damn it!
It's snowing again. These blasted English winters!
I want to go to South Africa with Venerable
Anando,'—now, that is something I have created
right now, just sitting here. I am not contemplating,
I am just reacting: 'It's snowing again, blast it!'
If I contemplate, however, I can be quite peaceful.
White snow on a bleak landscape is calming to the
mind. I can look out there and contemplate; it is
quite tranquillising, it does not excite; it is not a
stimulating landscape; it is all quite colourless and
subdued, quiet, silent. If, on the other hand, we
want interesting, fascinating life styles, we might
find all this a bit boring. We think: 'How boring
it is! White snow, few colours, no leaves on
the trees, no flowers in the garden, just kind of
colourless shades, sepia tones.' And then we think:
'Remember those beautiful, fascinating gardens
in Borneo—wild colours of orange, red and yel-
low—beautiful parrots in the trees, flamingoes.'
And then immediately we are sitting here in
the middle of an English winter—there are no
flamingoes! We are creating suffering because we
are thinking about something that is not here,

and resenting the fact. Now, as contemplators of life, we have to open up to this sepia-toned bleak English winter just like the inhalation and the exhalation.

I saw a film on an aeroplane, *Flash Dance*. It was the story of a lady. Whenever she heard a certain kind of music, her whole body started going all over the place, no matter where she was. If she heard this music, she just started leaping into the air. That kind of music can excite the mind. But mindfulness of breathing will not do that! It is a different kind of rhythm. Jungle rhythms are exciting; the body, the mind, gets all excited. I am not saying excitement is bad; do not misunderstand me. I am saying that that is what it is like. Mindfulness of breathing, however, is a tranquillising slow rhythm. And it is something we do not make up; we do not create it.

Now, if we are not feeling tranquil throughout this mindfulness of breathing, it is because we are expecting more from it than it can give us—we do not understand it yet, we are not really *giving* ourselves to it; we are just using it to get some state that we want. But when we start reflecting that mindfulness is about just being with an inhalation, just being with an exhalation, then it is its own reward. While we are concentrating on that, being aware of it, our minds for that moment are calm, even though our bodies may not be. But the more we calm the mind, the more the body calms. The body demands a lot of patience. From just little things like this, tremendous wisdom arises in our lives.

We could spend thirty years reading philosophy at Oxford University. We could read Bertrand Russell and all that—the head would be chock-a-block full of ideas, views and opinions. The brain would be bursting with information. I would say: 'Watch your breath.' You would say: 'Can't be bothered; a waste of time. I'm writing an important paper for an important journal.' If we look in the University archives, we shall see all the doctoral theses that have been written over the past one hundred years. All the hard work that has gone into writing those things, and the headaches and the anxiety and a lot of it is worthless! Now, we do not get PhDs for watching the breath. If I wanted to write a doctoral thesis on one inhalation, they would say: 'Don't be facetious, can't give you a PhD for that.'

If we find ourselves being overwhelmed by things in life, we can just take the time to use mindfulness of breathing. We should not use it to try to get out of things, but just as a place to compose ourselves. So, some exciting, difficult situation is happening around us—one inhalation! For that moment, at least, we can compose ourselves; we need not be whirled away by things that happen. It is a very useful thing to do, very skilful. It does take practice, however. We have to put forth the effort into going towards that mindfulness because it is not interesting enough to attract us. Jungle rhythms *will* attract us, but not mindfulness of breathing. That is the way it is. It does not attract, but it can tranquillise. Then, when we realise the result, get good results from mindfulness of breathing, *then* we shall find it attractive, *then* we shall *want* to do it; then we would rather go to that than to the jungle rhythm.

The mind can get scattered and dull, but just fifteen minutes, say, of concentrating on the breath can sharpen it up again. We can see where we tend to lose the mind; it is where it wanders. Then we can put forth a special effort to really hold the mind to an inhalation, to an exhalation. And that is a suppression of other things; we are suppressing all other sensory impingement in order to concentrate on one sensory impingement. But that is not an end in itself; it is merely a skilful means.

We can also listen to the sound of silence; and we can do that at the same time as being mindful of breathing. Now, if we notice, when our minds wander, we no longer hear the sound of silence. We forget about it and go off into thoughts and moods.

When our minds wander, there are ways of bringing our attention back to the moment. We can, however, become attached to ideas about these ways—the idea of emptiness, for example, or the idea of bringing ourselves back to the moment. Any idea we attach to will take us to doubt again. People say: 'Bring yourself back to the moment.' But that can become a fixation, an obsession, rather than a skilful composing of their minds. We are very keen on attaching to techniques, words, ideas, or to anything. We tend to say: 'Give me the formula, give me the technique, give me the magic word,' as if there was one magic word, or one technique which was going to do everything for us.

We should note the opinions that arise if any of these things become compulsive. We may tell ourselves to 'Let go! Let go!' Then soon we find ourselves using it for anything and everything; it becomes just a perfunctory, habitual statement. Something goes wrong—one of the buildings catches fire. We say: 'Let go!' and don't bother to report it because reporting a fire might mean we are attached to the idea of fire. That is the ultimate absurdity.

At Chithurst there used to be the 'watch your mind' habit. We would say: 'Watch your mind!' It was a way of saying: 'Shut up!' Something would go wrong in the kitchen, somebody would get upset and say: 'Watch your mind!' They were not watching theirs, obviously.

And yet all these things are skilful means— watching the mind and letting go. Letting go of 'the house on fire' does not mean we should not do anything about it; it does not mean we just pretend it does not exist—that would be impossible. It would be very foolish too. We 'let go of fire' by following the insight into doing what is *appropriate* at that moment.

Some people do not know the difference between 'mindfulness' and 'concentration'. They concentrate on what they are doing, thinking that is being mindful. I knew someone once who was always complaining about other people not being mindful. He would be absorbed in what he was doing and then perhaps someone would go and ask him a question and he would blow up, have a temper tantrum! Now, he *could* concentrate. We can concentrate on what we are doing, but if we are not mindful at the same time, with the ability to reflect on the moment, then if somebody interferes with our concentration, we may blow up, get carried away by anger at being frustrated. If we are mindful, we are aware of the tendency to first concentrate and then to feel anger when something interferes with that concentration. With mindfulness we can concentrate when it is appropriate to do so and not concentrate when it is appropriate not to do so. If we are concentrating on what we are doing and then something else happens, we can reflect on how to solve that other problem, or do that other thing, without getting into a terrible state about it and without upsetting others.

Reflecting is being mindful. Yesterday is the past, a memory. Tomorrow is the unknown. This is the moment. Reflecting is bringing into consciousness the way things are—we are sitting here; we are aware of our intentions; we are aware of what is going on and of what is happening inside ourselves; we are aware of anything influencing us, like a feeling of anger with somebody; we observe any feelings of resistance. Sometimes we do not want to do something—we observe it all. That is mindfulness, being aware of the forces that are being experienced, externally and internally, emotionally and physically.

We can also be aware of assumptions. We may have idealistic natures so that we are always thinking about how things *should* be, wanting everything to be the way it *should* be, not wanting anything to be as it should not be, not wanting anything to get in our way or frustrate us, not wanting to hear bad news, not wanting to have

problems, quarrels or disharmony, wanting everybody to be happy and grateful and devoted! We
can learn a lot about ourselves through all this. We
can learn because we can reflect on the way things
happen to be, now.

We do not feel exactly the same every day at
this time, do we? Things change, like the weather.
There may be an emergency. Somebody has to
go to the hospital, or somebody comes suddenly,
and we say: 'Let go!' We can adapt according to
change, rather than rigidly try to make everything
a certain way. This does not mean we become
wishy-washy, just going all over the place without
any kind of starch in the material, without any
real strength, to the point where we say: 'Oh, I'm
learning to adapt to everything,' so that when we
feel a bit tired, we crash down on the floor: 'I'm
just learning to adapt to tiredness.' If we do not
have any strength, if we do not observe how things
are, but just have ideas of letting go, we can be
very fixed. Ideals can make us very rigid beings.
Instead of being rather wishy-washy, we may be so
resolute that we become downright stubborn and
difficult. Then we become insensitive, troublesome

nuisances. Yet somebody who does not have any resolutions at all, just floats about in the wind.

The Buddhist way is a way of 'no fixed position'. There is no position that one takes as a Buddhist. That is a strange one isn't it? We are not asked to believe in Buddha, there is no *for* or *against,* no *affirming* or *denying.* We watch any attachments to Buddhism. We may think: 'Buddhism is the best!' Or: 'It's probably worthless.' From the ideal position we may think: 'I shouldn't have any opinions at all; one shouldn't have opinions or views.' But that is another opinion. Having no fixed position is not another position, but a reflection on any position. It is a great relief to the heart, really, not to feel that we have to know everything or have everything, and not to have to defend our actions. I have found myself being very defensive about my way of life, trying to justify it, trying to make people understand, trying to prove that it is right. Some opinions may be right, some wrong, but when we grasp them as absolutely right or absolutely wrong, then we are deluded by them.

Grasping, trying to make absolutes out of relative truths, makes everything go wrong. We need to know what is absolute and what is relative, what is ultimate reality and what is relative reality. By fixing on a particular doctrine, for example, we make what is relative into an absolute. And because it can never be absolute, we have to defend it, try to convince ourselves and everyone else that it is so. I say: 'This is absolutely true and you'd better believe it.' And someone else says: 'No, it's not; it's only relative.' And I say: 'IT'S TRUE! IT'S ABSOLUTELY TRUE!' My voice gets louder to drown him out because he is putting a doubt into my mind. Then someone else agrees with me: 'Venerable Sumedho, that's absolutely true! You're absolutely right!' 'Good, good. He agrees with me.' Then I say: 'Don't talk to that other person because he might put doubts into your mind.'

Once we have a fixed view, we can get ourselves so deeply involved, it just mushrooms into enormous problems. If we do not have a fixed position and yet find ourselves attaching to viewpoints and arguing about them, then we can reflect on the anxiety and insecurity which arises when someone threatens our position. The skilful thing is not to argue, because we are just spouting views and opinions that other people have given us.

Ideals can, of course, be used skilfully as guides, goals and inspiration, but as soon as we attach to any of them, then we are fixed. And what happens when we are fixed to even the highest ideal? We become critical of ourselves and others. We talk about universal compassion: 'We must have compassion for all sentient beings.' Then somebody annoys me, and I say: 'Shut up and get out of here!' Sometimes it is easier to have compassion for all sentient beings than for one annoying one.

Why is that? Because ideals are not emotions; they are high-minded and refined. Our emotions can be very coarse. To have compassion for a mass of people we are never likely to meet—there is no emotion in that, there is no threat. But if millions of people were to suddenly come and live here at this centre, then it would be a real trial! To have to feel compassion for millions of them all squeezing in might bring about a few uncompassionate thoughts and feelings! As long as they remain over there, it is easy. So, we can feel compassion for all beings and the next moment want to murder someone. The ideal is still there, even in the mind that wants to murder. Ideals, you see, do not have blood in their veins. Millions of people we are unlikely to meet are not people with blood in their veins. The person threatening us with a knife—that is someone with real blood in his veins, and we have real blood in ours that can get very disturbed and violent.

If we reflect in this way, we get a perspective into hypocrisy. I have seen it in myself. A fixed view: 'I'm right! I'm right! The other's wrong!' And I have to prove I am right; I will not give an inch. That kind of position just breeds conflict. All I can do is try to drag people into agreeing with me and try to defend myself against those who do not agree. What is that? That is a war, isn't it? And usually it is about some unimportant thing. I decided some time ago that there was no point in spending my life trying to do that any more—it seemed to be just an endless thing, endless opportunities for conflict in the sensual world. One day I decided it would be better to live a moral life and not to make problems about things. There are certain things worth standing up for and upholding even to the death, and there are other things that are not worth the bother. And yet we can spend our lives trying to defend not very important things.

By reflecting, we can see our own weaknesses. This takes honesty and truthfulness; we have to be willing to look at our own fears and anxieties. There are warning signs, of course. As soon as I feel depressed, negative, worried, frightened, anxious, that is the messenger sent to warn me of attachment. Old age is also a warning sign, and sickness, weakness, pain. When someone dies, that is a warning sign. These are heavenly messengers, warning us. A wise person will heed these warnings, will go right to the feeling itself.

Taking a Stand

At Wat Pah Pong in Thailand we used to spend hours out in the hot sun, the boiling hot sun in the afternoon, sweeping the leaves. It was really unpleasant to have that sun on you. We had to make our own brooms. We would get a long bamboo pole, some strips of bamboo and branches, and then put the strips of bamboo around the branches to hold them onto the pole. If you were really good at it, you could make a very nice broom with a kind of spring to it. And once you became an expert, sweeping leaves was very pleasant. But I considered it to be totally unimportant and unnecessary. I did not put any effort into learning how to make a decent broom—just went through the motions because I had to, and because I knew I would be criticised if I did not. So I would go out there with a broom that was no good and just go through the motions of sweeping. I hated the whole thing, complained inwardly, went on like a little brat: 'I'm fed up with this; don't want to do this. After all, I came here to study the Buddha's teaching and to practise, and here I am just sweeping leaves to no purpose . . . in the hot sun . . . blah, blah, blah.' I had this kind of awful character in me; he was called 'the whining complainer'. I looked at the other monks and thought: 'They're just rice farmers. They're stupid illiterate boys from paddy fields; they'll just do what they're told.' I was talking to myself: 'I am so intelligent and so gifted and such a great gift to the monastery, how could they possibly expect me to carry on like this?'

One day I was going through the motions, really depressed, and Ajahn Chah came along. He smiled and said: 'Where is the suffering? Is Wat Pah Pong a lot of suffering?' It was just the right thing to say. Suddenly I understood very clearly and realised what an indulgent, childish, foolish, little brat I was at thirty-two! I thought: 'You know this is all right—sweeping leaves. Wat Pah Pong is all right. People are nice. The Ajahn is wise. The sun is

bearable. I'm not all that bad. I'm not dying; I'm not getting sick from it.' Then I realised what misery I had created in my mind. And I started reflecting: 'I can do this job; it's really not much of a request at all. They don't expect very much from me here, and yet what they do ask me to do, I complain about.' I saw what a really unpleasant kind of person I could be, and yet I had considered myself to be quite a good person actually. I had been blaming the other monks, blaming Ajahn Chah, not liking the sun, not liking the leaves, not liking the broom, not wanting to be bothered about making a decent broom and so having to scratch the ground with a miserable little thing. If I had made a nice broom with a good spring to it, I could have got some wonderful sweeps; with one swipe I could have got all the leaves to go in a nice way and make lovely piles. The soil was sandy, so it was possible to get nice sweeping patterns in the sand. I began to quite enjoy it—the aesthetic quality of it, and the pleasure of just using the body. When the mind was right, the other was right. Before that I had just wanted to sit and meditate on my own terms, which I found quite easy to do, and which I could really enjoy. When asked to do something which I did not like, I created miserable thoughts.

We can reflect on the suffering of life. Where is that suffering? Now, does it arise? Where does it end? Yesterday is a memory; tomorrow is the unknown; now is the knowing—this is the pattern of reflection. Now is the knowing. Sitting in meditation, what is the mood? What is the feeling? This is the time.

It takes a lot of wisdom to live rightly. If we take the world for granted and never reflect on it, then of course we are carried to old age, sickness, death, despair and anguish. Bodies are all getting older. Just reflecting on age, without getting carried away by the thought, without indulging in it—what is it like? 'Fifty years old.' What is my perception of being fifty? And what is the physical feeling of a body that is fifty? Often there is a great discrepancy between the mind and body. The mind is still thirty and the body is fifty!

Moreover we can have an idea of what a man is and of what a woman is. The modern trend is that there should not be any differences. Men say:

'Women take advantage of every situation—try to get the upper hand, use their charm to manipulate men and get anything they want; and then they want everything else! Not only do they use their feminine wiles, but they also want the advantages of masculinity. They're just insatiably greedy, ungrateful wretches!' Then the feminist movement goes on about how God is a man; how everything that is good is named masculine; how men dominate, are aggressive, get higher wages, and have completely humiliated women throughout the ages to the ultimate degree! One can justify both positions.

When you take a fixed position, however, then you see all the faults of the other side, because the fixed position does not allow you to see in perspective, or to understand yourself at all. But in the 'knowing', in awareness, we recognise the position we happen to be taking. It is not that we cannot take positions, but that we recognise what we are doing. We recognise, perhaps, that sometimes we are just frightened of men or of women. We can get a lot of energy by hating or taking a strong stand against something, without understanding what we are doing. And we can become fanatical.

Reflection is the recognition that that is the way it is. We do not have to understand in a rational way. We begin to give space in the mind for all conditions to arise and pass away, whether they are intellectual, rational, sensible, thoroughly understandable, or just emotional. We open the mind to the way it is, not to the way *I* want it to be. Even though we may be fully mature—the body may be thirty, sixty, eighty—the emotions could still be childish. We begin to listen to 'the whining complainer', the frightened little child. When we cannot get on with someone, we tend to feel frightened or threatened by that person. Then we tend to have bad thoughts about him and be jealous of him. We can bring that up into consciousness. We can hear it: 'He's this way; he's that way. I can't stand the way he does this. I don't like the way he does that.' When we are obsessed with aversion, or fear of someone, it is important to go to the place where that feeling arises.

If you live alone, it is possible to get away with a lot; you can live on your own terms. But in a community things are thrown back at you very quickly. From my own experience, being in a position of authority, I notice that some people are just very frightened of me, which used to surprise me. I would think: 'I've a good heart, I've a very kind heart. I wouldn't hurt a fly, and yet some people seem to be absolutely terrified of me.' Then someone would say: 'Well, it's the way you look. You know, you have a very stern look sometimes. You're big, and you have this stern look—it's absolutely frightening! 'Well, I did not know that. I cannot see myself. I do not look big to myself and I do not feel stern, yet that is how other people see me. So I listen to that. I watch the results of my presence on others, rather than just blindly going through life wondering why people act the way they do 'when I haven't done anything—always tried my hardest—work hard, kind heart, nobody fully appreciating me.' And I think they must be bad people because I am certainly all right! But, you know, even though we may have golden hearts, sometimes we have very annoying habits! So I put some effort into not annoying others out of heedlessness, and I try to live in a way that is helpful to those around me, not becoming obsessed by it, but reflecting and learning. And I see that I do actually have some annoying traits that maybe I can change if I am more careful, more considerate.

If something is always coming back at you in a community, then you really have to investigate it. Sometimes it is just the constant little annoying habits that drive people up the wall, really get under their skins. Somebody does the same foolish thing over and over and over again, and you think: 'Say, stop it!' And then you think: 'Well, I'll learn to be more patient.' I have learned to be very patient with a lot of very annoying things, which is good for me. But also, in a community, we try to live in a way which is more skilful. We do not really know the effect we are having on others. Sometimes we do not care! Someone has a terrible annoying habit. I am really upset and I say: 'Shut up and watch your mind!' That is the meditator's way of saying: 'Drop dead!' To become obsessed with not being annoyed, or to become obsessed with trying to please everybody, is one extreme. The other extreme is not to care what others think and not to put any effort into doing other than just what one wants to do. These are the two extremes—to say: 'Watch your mind! Drop dead!' or to say: 'Oh, I'm sorry, did I? I hope I didn't do anything to upset you. Oh, I try so hard not to offend anybody.' We can listen to these forces in ourselves. I can listen to that in me which is callous and insensitive and wants to say: 'Don't bother me! Get lost!' I can also hear the thing in me that wants to say: 'I hope I'm not hurting anyone. I hope I'm not doing anything to offend anyone here. I hope I haven't done anything to upset you.' To reflect on these two extremes is to make conscious these very feelings.

Being male or female, young or old, middle-aged, American, English, Swiss, French, Spanish, whatever, these are what we reflect on. We can watch and learn from these conditions. Being the Abbot of a monastery is an important position in worldly terms. So I reflect on those terms without identifying or attaching to them. To say: 'I'm the Abbot of a monastery,' is appropriate at certain times and in certain situations. It is not an absolute, though; it is not a person. If we are really stupid we shall hold on to a qualification as a kind of fixed identity. And then we become rigid, foolish types of beings. There is nothing more unpleasant than seeing someone always carrying his qualifications around with him, and imposing them on every situation for personal advantage.

Then there is the other extreme: 'I'm nobody. I'm just nobody. I'm . . . just a monk of no importance. I've no special qualities; I'm not President, not in charge of anything, just a junior insignificant nothing.' That is really another way of boasting. I say I do not boast about being this or that because I know I am just an insignificant nobody of no importance. But I am proud of that! And then there are those with the kind of mentality that resents authority and always has to knock it down, because, for them, people with authority are a threat, while people at the bottom, without authority, are no threat. 'There's the *really* humble one, the one at the end, the one without *anything.*' This tendency is in us. When reflecting we can observe the positioning of beings in relationship to us, this hierarchical structure, not justifying or condemning it, but observing it as a condition of the mind, and then being aware of the sense of self in relationship to others. It is not that we should have certain reflections, and not have others, but we should know them for what they are. Whatever arises passes away and is not self. That is how to skilfully use the situations we are in, whether sitting, standing, walking, lying down, working, or drinking tea!

It's Not Fair

A woman came to the monastery once with a sick baby. The baby was in great agony. She said: 'Why does this sweet little boy have to suffer? He hasn't hurt anyone. He has trouble breathing and he nearly died. Why does he have to suffer? What did he do to deserve this?' I said: 'He was born! You wanted to have a baby; the baby was born, it got sick.' That was not being cold-hearted or brutal; it was pointing to the truth. What did the little boy do to deserve that sickness? If we want to make a personal assessment, we can speculate: 'Maybe in a previous life he stepped on a caterpillar!' But that is speculation. What we actually know is that he was born and birth means being subject to pain. These bodies are *going* to feel pain; they are going to get illnesses; they are *going* to get old; they are going to die.

Admittedly, some people are more inclined to sickness than others, but we all have our share of it and we shall all get old and die. We could say: 'What did I do to deserve this? Why do I have to suffer?' 'What did she do to deserve cancer? She's always given to charity. She's a good mother, a good wife. She's kind. But she's got cancer! Why? It's not fair! Only old biddies, selfish, mean, nasty old bags, should get cancer! Nice good-hearted ladies like this one shouldn't get it.' 'Why should the innocent suffer? If we want things to be fair, only the guilty should suffer. As in a war—it's fair, if only the bad ones suffer—those who start the wars and support them. If *they* suffer, then it's all right. But in wars most of those who suffer aren't the ones who start them—the ones who suffer are those who just happen to be in the wrong place at the wrong time—innocent bystanders, women and children and all those who'd like the war to end. IT'S NOT FAIR.'

We were all glad when Hitler was done in; he was such a bad lot. Everybody rejoiced when he died. But a lot of innocent, very nice people can die too, in terrible ways, being tortured and brutalised—why? Why does this happen? Because they were born! We were all born and are therefore open to the possibility of being tortured. A Buddhist monk, living under the rules of the Order for twenty years, could be kidnapped by a terrorist organisation and tortured to death in the most horrendous way. What did he do to deserve it? It was the result of birth.

Contemplating in this way, we no longer whine about things not being fair, and why the world has to be *this* way. It is not that we justify the crime and atrocities that beings experience; it is merely an acceptance of the fact that this is the way it is. If we do not accept the way things are, then we create suffe ring. We worry, blame, condemn, and create all kinds of misery in our minds, simply because the world is not the way we would like it to be.

A body is born into the world as a separate being. It is conscious; there are sense organs; there are feelings. Even the newest baby feels; it feels hunger, cold, heat and so forth. Its feelings are not developed all that much, still, it definitely feels—instinctual feeling, sensory feeling. However, a baby does not seem to have any concept of a self. Most babies I know do not seem to have a 'self' view. They do not think 'I am' until they are older.

I have a sister two years older than myself and I remember feeling very unhappy when she did not want to take baths with me any more. I did not understand the difference between boys and girls at that time and we used to have lots of fun in the bathtub, my sister and I—innocent fun. But then she reached an age when she refused to take baths with me, and I could not understand why. I thought she was just being difficult, or perhaps did not like me any more. But actually she was developing a sense of 'I am a girl and he's a boy' with the resultant feelings.

When a baby is born, it has no sense of being male or female, does it? It does not think: 'I am a boy', or 'I am a girl'. That sort of thing is conditioned into it later on. The mind is conditioned according to culture, family, class and the times we live in. All of the conditioning is added, instilled into the mind; it is something which is not the mind itself: 'Little boys should be *this* way; little girls should be *that* way.' We get all kinds of suggestions from our families and peers about ourselves and begin to think: 'I'm a good boy. I'm clever,' or: 'I'm stupid.' These are suggestions that we get from the people around us. And we form the 'self' view. Because we are naughty and do certain things parents say: 'You're a bad boy!' There is this little rhyme I remember from when I was a child: *Girls are made of sugar and spice and everything nice. Boys are made of frogs and snails and puppydogs' tails.* And I certainly remember feeling quite put out about that! I liked sugar and spice.

Little boys were supposed to be difficult and little girls were supposed to be sweet, good, obedient. These were the perceptions I acquired from that early part of my childhood. Maybe it is true! Still, the 'self' view is formed by all these little rhymes, old wives' tales, and cultural attitudes.

When we meditate we begin to realise the mind itself, where there is no condition, where there is no sense of 'I am', 'I am a boy', 'I am a girl'. In meditation we can notice what the unconditioned mind is. As unawakened individuals we tend to not notice this; we are just caught in the reactions of 'I am *this;*' 'I am *that;*' 'I *should* be . . . ; 'I *shouldn't* be . . . ' And we go around with the 'I am', believing it to be true and real—the 'real world'. To live in the 'real world' is to do what is considered normal by the society or class into which we have been born. But in meditation, mental formations and conceptualisations, cease in the mind. And we do not dissolve into thin air! We do not become unconscious! Nothing has been annihilated! And we can reflect on this fact. What does take place is a cessation of the conditioned world—that which arises.

This is the practice of 'letting the world cease'. What is left is awareness, mindfulness, knowing. And that, we say, is not an 'I am'; it is not a 'self'; it is not 'a personal quality'; and it is no more 'mine' than it is 'yours'. When there is nongrasping and awareness, the mind is not 'my' mind or 'your' mind. 'Boys' and 'girls' arise and cease *in* the mind. If we look into a mirror, of course, we may still think of ourselves as our bodies: '*My* appearance, *my* body—this is me; this is *my* face. Would you like a picture of me? I'll

give you a picture of my face. That's me . . .'
But in awareness we do not think that much about
the body in the sense of it being 'me' and 'mine'.
So the body as being 'me' and 'mine' ceases in
the mind.

When we practise mindfulness of breathing, we
do not think: 'This is *my* inhalation and this is
my exhalation.' Trying to keep the 'me' going in
respect to our breathing would drive us crazy;
it would be absurd. Breathing is not a self, but
breathing is going on—bodies are breathing. If we
think: 'I'm breathing,' then somebody is born who
is breathing. When there is no such thought, there
is still breathing, but nobody is doing it. It is a
kind of paradox. These bodies breathe; it is their
nature to do so. Whether we think the body is ours
or not, whether we are aware of it or not, it is
still breathing because that is its nature. As long
as it is alive, it breathes. The thought 'I breathe'
is something we create. To say 'I breathe' is just
a statement—a statement, however, fraught with a
sense of 'me' and mine.

When I was a child I was asthmatic and I
remember how difficult it was to breathe. There

was real panic as I tried to catch my breath. 'I can't breathe any more!' I used to turn blue. My mother would go into a panic. She said I could turn blue instantaneously. The sense of 'me', 'I can't breathe,' 'I want to breathe,' arose. But when there was no problem with asthma, when the breathing was normal, then there was not a self. Natural functions are not persons. And yet we create all kinds of problems around them—around eating, around sexual desire, excretory functions, even perspiration.

In the Victorian days women were not supposed to sweat; it was unladylike. There were all kinds of perceptions that somehow sweating was a vulgar and disgusting thing to do. Men could get away with it, but not women. People were attached to the perception that femininity was something refined, with nothing coarse about it whatsoever. So a coarse, unpleasant aspect of the human body had to be suppressed and rejected. That was a cultural perception, a hangup of Victorian Britain a hundred years ago.

The common attitude these days is that we should have a good ego before we practise insight meditation—we should have a highly developed ego, then we can let it go. People have spoken to me about this. They think I should not be teaching the doctrine of no-self because the egos of some of us have not developed to the point yet where we can let them go. But I am not trying to destroy anyone's ego. What I am saying is that whether we have a positive view of ourselves or not, the ego is just a conditioned thing. To accept—rather than to judge—even a wretched ego, can only help. It can only help to accept it, rather than to feel we should be trying to look upon ourselves as the *best* instead of the *worst.*

Sometimes people will come and say: 'I've realised my true nature. I'm wonderful! I'm a miracle of God! I'm beautiful and lovable, and I'm the happiest, the most wonderful person.' When people make statements like that, it makes me wonder what they are really trying to say. To go around talking like that is just the opposite of saying: 'Oh, I'm a hopeless case, a failure. I'm an unlovable old tramp and I can't see how anyone could possibly like me.' There are those of the view that we should think the best of ourselves, that we should think of ourselves as absolutely wonderful, lovable, beautiful creatures. But I have learned a lot from thinking of myself as hopeless, from seeing the ego, not as something to develop and grasp at, but as something to understand and know. And from that understanding a sense of self-respect has come about. I am not trying to convince myself that I am an absolutely wonderful man, but I do respect myself because I live in a way that I respect, and I try to do things and act in a way that I find I *can* respect. So, as an individual being, as a monk, as this being here, I respect it; I do not feel ashamed or averse to it. Really that is an ego, but it is not an ego in the sense that I have to think about myself in a positive way, to go from thinking that I am a hopeless case to thinking that I am the most wonderful creature on the planet. It is not an ego in the sense of affirmations of self or negations of self. 'No-self' does not mean annihilation of a self; it means seeing self for what it is and no longer identifying with it, or clinging to a 'self' view.

As we realise a state of being awake and calm, we can contemplate: 'Is there a self?' And we can be aware that 'self' is the ability to reflect on the way it is—not judging, not criticising, not creating anything, but just observing, noticing. We can be aware of the 'I am' arising—what 'I' think, what 'I' feel, what 'I' want; 'If you want my opinion ...' These are concepts that arise and cease in the mind and we can observe them.

I used to take the 'I am' and just listen to it. I would call it 'the space around "I am"' and with deliberate intention think: 'I AM.' Before I thought it, I would notice that there was no thought there. Then I would think: 'I AM.' That is so simple, but we do not notice it; we do not notice that before the 'I am' there is nobody. There is awareness, there is mindfulness, there is an intention in the mind to think, but there is no thought. Then the thought 'I am' arises, and then it ceases.

We are pointing at the emptiness rather than at the thought, at the mind wherein the 'I am' arises and ceases, rather than at the condition of 'I am'. In this way we see 'I am' in perspective; it is neither an obsession nor a habit-formation. 'I am a Buddhist monk;' 'I am a wonderful man;' 'I am a hopeless case!' These all arise and then cease.

I used to deliberately think all the worst possible thoughts: 'What can I think that's the worst possible thing to think?' And then I would think it. It would arise and cease in the mind. 'What is the best, the highest, the most altruistic, the finest thought that a human being can possibly think?' And that would also arise and cease. As an experiment, we can take thoughts—the worst and the best—with the deliberate intention of examining and investigating our reactions to them.

'I shouldn't think bad thoughts, I should only think good ones.' And then we would have bad thoughts and think: 'I shouldn't be thinking like this. I wish I didn't have these kinds of thoughts; I wish I were someone who had beautiful thoughts; I wish I were a loving person with a generous heart; I wish I could be just full of love and joy, but instead I'm frightened and jealous, get angry, upset, have bad thoughts and it's terrible . . . !' And this goes around and around. 'What's wrong with me that I should be like this?' This is a case of being caught in the whirlpool of 'self' again, isn't it?

When we look at thought itself, the finest as

well as the meanest, it just arises and ceases. We can notice the space, the empty mind, rather than the thought. And we do not have to make anything out of thought. It can be seen as a condition that begins and ends. This is one way of really getting to know the emptiness of mind, the mind that is clear and bright and not personal, not 'me', not 'mine', not a man or a woman, not clean or dirty, not high or low, not good or bad. To realise this is to abide more and more in emptiness, less and less in thought.

We may be angry with somebody: 'He said *that* to me and I'll never forgive him!' 'And then last week, you know what he did?' 'And last year, five years ago, you know what he did?' The mind just connects with all the bad things that that person had done. The anger stimulates these thoughts. But when we like that person again, we love them: 'I really love you; you're wonderful.' And the person says: 'But you know what I did last week?' And we say: 'Oh, never mind, it's nothing really. Don't even mention it!'

When we love somebody we do not want to remember the bad things he or she has done; we want to go along with the nice things and the good things. When we are in love and somebody is critical of the person we are in love with, we do not want to hear. We say: 'Go away! Get lost!' But if someone comes along and talks about how wonderful that person is, we are just so happy: 'Your friend is a wonderful person who's really sensitive. You know what she did last week? She helped an old lady across the street.' 'That's my sweetheart—a *wonderful* person.' We find ourselves having memories of something that happened before, a kind of *déjà vu* experience, because of this ability to associate and remember.

If we are great thinkers and like to study logic, we have a particular way of thinking, a particular jargon that we use. We may hear sociologists talking about 'patrilineal' and 'matrilineal' this and that societies. It does not mean much to anyone who is not a sociologist; it is just a jargon which that particular discipline has developed. It is conditioned into the mind and is associative. Within the conventions of the jargon, the mind goes from one concept to the next. However, all of the thoughts arise and cease—and this is what unawakened people do not notice. It is not that they are thinking all the time; it is just that they do not notice when they are *not* thinking; they are only conscious through thought.

The thought 'I am' and the absorption into conditions makes us feel alive. When there is nothing happening, most of us are not really conscious any more; we do not feel alive; we are not absorbed into anything, and we kind of float around in a fog. So we look for something to absorb into, something interesting, pleasant, sensual, exciting, something to make us feel alive again, something which will lead to our being reborn again as a person. The unawakened, ignorant human being is constantly having to be reborn. And that rebirth takes place through sensual pleasures, through becoming something, or through getting rid of something.

Asceticism, for example, is the 'self' that feels alive when it is being tortured, when it is being denied something. There is a strong sense of self in that: 'I feel alive when I'm fasting and when I'm on my bed of nails . . . my hair shirt and the whip . . . Beat me so that I can feel alive!' You wonder about sadomasochists—why people do things like that. It is probably because it makes them feel alive. If nobody is persecuting them, nobody is paying attention to them. If nobody is beating them and they do not have a bed of nails, a hair shirt, something nice to eat, or something interesting to do, then they tend to fall asleep! The realms of stimulation are very important to such people.

Why do so many of us watch these soap operas on the television? It is because we actually *become* these people. A successful film will absorb our attention so that we forget ourselves; we forget everything and become completely absorbed into the story.

We can notice the subtlety when we pay attention to where there is no self, to where there is silence, stillness and calm. When we begin to appreciate the realisation of emptiness, it becomes our natural inclination; we feel more peaceful and at ease at being with the way things are—the breathing of the body, the silence.

Because of physical birth there is breathing, feeling, and consciousness; there is also sickness and ageing, and there will be death. One thing leads on from another. Because there are eyes, there is eye-consciousness. It is not a personal thing. We can reflect on eye-consciousness, contemplate it, reflect on what eye-consciousness is, rather than just reacting: 'Oh, look at that beautiful Buddha-rupa!' That is a reaction as the eye contacts the Buddha-rupa. We think: 'Oh, I'd really like that Buddha-rupa; that's beautiful.' And then we start looking: 'Oh, look at those flowers.' 'Look, they still haven't washed the curtains in this place yet!' But when we contemplate eye-consciousness, we can observe that there is just consciousness. There is then no question of thinking of the Buddha-rupa as being beautiful or ugly, or of thinking about the flowers, or of thinking that the curtains need washing—criticising. We do not perceive what we see as actually being anything; we do not make any comment, or judge it, or call it anything. Then we can perceive it as . . . a box, a blue box. That is a reflection on consciousness.

The sense of 'I am' says: 'This is *my* box.' I may just make the assumption that you put this box here for me, and if someone takes it away I say: 'You can't have *my* box—get your own!' But really, to say: 'This is my box, not yours,' is a convention. The unawakened mind, operating from an assumption of a self, assumes that the box belongs to 'me' in a kind of absolute way. In reflective meditation we look at such assumptions; we contemplate the way things are, so that we can be wise and clear, so that we are not deluded by what happens and get caught in immature reactions, fears, and desires.

It is like getting a cold. It could be a form of suffering: 'I don't want a cold; I hate colds; I want to get rid of it.' Or it could be a reflection. We can contemplate the fact that colds happen sometimes as a result of being born as a human being. Human beings catch colds. That is a reflection on the way things are—not a judgement, not blaming anybody or taking it personally.

We can really look at the 'I am'. We can practise listening to the space around the thought, to the silence. What do we have to do to notice the space in this room? We must take our attention off the objects. If we focus on an object, then we absorb into it and are not aware of space until we attend to space. We need to contemplate space and form, and use them as visual experiences, or as mental experiences. We can see thought and we can see emptiness—'I am' and emptiness—form and space. We can notice when there is no self and we can notice when there is self. Self arises and ceases, it is not absolute, there is no permanent self; self is 'self' views. 'I am' is merely a condition that comes and goes according to other conditions.

An Ugly Sand Grain

When we are not alert we tend to get caught up in the momentum of our habits. Worry is the big one, isn't it? To worry a lot drives people crazy. People also believe that if they are not worrying, they are not being responsible—'worrying means caring'. But worry is just the result of obsessive thought.

When we are alert we put energy into the mind. It is the same with the body. To hold the body upright takes energy, effort. Where does that effort come from? When the body dies, it falls apart, decays, disintegrates. No one can put effort into a corpse because the life force has gone. The life force is something filling out the body; it is a mental energy which docs not come from the body itself. We can fill the body with energy. We can also fill the mind with energy and be alert, attentive.

In the moment of alertness, there is no thought. Unless I deliberately want to think of something right now, there is no thought. There is alertness. I can see people in front of me and I can talk, but there is no worry about anything right now—no fear, no lust, no doubt—just the recognition of the moment. Now, if I am heedless, my mind starts wandering this way and that, taking things personally, feeling averse, feeling greedy, thinking: 'I don't want to give a talk; I want to go to sleep. Fed up with giving talks!' But if I empty the mind, then there is awareness of the situation and a relating to what is useful and valuable at this moment.

We start meditating by making life very simple for ourselves—taking the moral precepts and being mindful of breathing. We see the habit of the mind, wanting to talk, wanting to eat and drink. We tie ourselves up in morality, awareness of breathing, and silence. Then we begin to relax within that restriction. We begin to surrender to the limitations, the boundaries. What happens when we give up to these limitations? We feel peaceful, much more peaceful than if we dance and sing and allow desires to pull us this way and that. Being limited to watching the body and the sensations, and then just being awake and aware, is enough. Aware of what? Of the moment. At first we have an object of awareness—we can watch the breath or sensations within the body. And then we just attend to what is happening within the moment. We are moving towards letting go, ultimate simplicity, Nirvana, unconditioned realisation.

Suddenly all the rubbish of our lives starts taking a conscious form. Many of us like to think of ourselves as rather sensible, rational human beings—at least I do! 'A sensible and reasonable man—kindly, good-natured!' But we get caught up in foolishness, stupidity, irrationality, emotion, and really we are just downright rubbish! We cannot always be rational and sensible. To be able to do that we would have to keep rejecting anything that was not sensible, wouldn't we? But we do not want to know about all the rubbish that appears, preferring to turn to something interesting or exciting. In the restricted situation of morality, awareness, and silence, the image of being totally sensible and rational is difficult to maintain. The irrational, repressed rubbish surfaces. Surprising, isn't it? We did not know it was there. Our lives had been so conditioned, so managed and controlled, that the rubbishy side had not been seen, or if it had been seen, had immediately been turned away from: 'I want nothing to do with that!' When the rubbish starts surfacing, it is to be taken as a good sign. We should not act on the rubbish, however, nor repress it, nor follow it. We should observe it—fear, foolishness, stupidity, irrational feelings, repressed anger, and all the rubbish that we might have previously repressed; we can become fully conscious of it all, which means that we have a way of letting it go rather than of pushing it back. Our meditation, then, can sometimes be just peacefully coexisting with a chattering mind, with stupidity, with irrational thinking. We just patiently watch it as a silent witness. We are not watching a self; it is not a personal thing; it is just a series of conditions that have never been allowed to become conscious.

In the past, conditions which had never been allowed to become conscious had always been stored away. In other words, they still had their karmic force, they still affected us. When we allow these conditions to take conscious form, then the karmic force ends. This means that we free ourselves from the burden of that repressed karmic force. We no longer hold anything back and run away, but allow ourselves to see conditions. These conditions are not seen as personal things; we do not see some corny, maniacal being!

The mind is like a mirror; it has the ability to reflect things. Mirrors reflect anything—beautiful or ugly, good or bad. And those things do not harm the mirror. No matter what the mirror reflects, the mirror is all right. Reflections pass in front of the mirror. They are there—and then they go. They are not the mirror itself. No matter how hideous or horrid the reflections might be, they are only reflections and we need not punish the mirror.

We must be very patient, willing to endure the smell of rubbish until it passes away. A skilful way of enduring the unpleasant, that which we tend to be averse to or frightened of, is by loving-kindness. The practice of loving-kindness is a skilful means. Now, this kind of love is kindly endurance. We usually use the word 'love' interchangeably with the word 'like' as though it were the same thing.

If we like something, we often say we love it. But in this practice of loving-kindness, we do not necessarily have to like a thing—we just do not feel any aversion for it. This is more like 'love' in the Christian sense of the word; it is an acceptance of a situation, without any dwelling on what is wrong, without dwelling on any flaw. Loving-kindness is the ability to be kind and gentle with that which we do not like.

It is easy to be kind and gentle with that which we do like—not difficult, quite pleasant. As far as people are concerned, it is difficult being nasty to those we like, whereas it may not be at all difficult to be nasty to those we do not like! The same with things or conditions. Some ugly, nasty thing appears in our minds. We think: 'I hate that. Get out of here!' That is not loving-kindness, is it? But if some ugly, nasty thing appears in our minds and we apply kindness, we can then accept it consciously and let it go. We do not hit it, have a go at it, and get upset by its presence. So, loving-kindness is a skilful way of enduring what we would not normally endure.

First of all, we must start practising loving-kindness with ourselves. If we hate ourselves, we tend to hate others. And any kindness we might feel for others is only superficial sentimentality. It is not real kindness because it comes from an idea. We establish loving-kindness with ourselves by not creating burdens out of what we have done in the past. Nor do we create burdens out of the foolishness of our thoughts, or our opinions and views. No guilt is created, no remorse or self-hatred. We can even practise loving-kindness for the pain in our bodies when we sit for a long time in meditation. This is kindness towards pain, not an aversion towards it, or wanting to get rid of it, or worrying about it. We may make a mistake, perhaps say something wrong, and instead of feeling guilty about it and hating ourselves, we can forgive ourselves for having weaknesses—not justifying them, but not creating problems around them either. Having a kindly patience towards the rubbish in our minds is a willingness to allow the unpleasant to exist, a willingness to allow it to take its natural course to cessation.

When we have loving-kindness for ourselves, we can have loving-kindness for others. We can exist with others without having aversion for those who are not very nice or whom we do not approve of. Without loving-kindness, we may think: 'I wish they wouldn't be that way—wish they wouldn't do that.' But when we have loving-kindness, we can endure the problems of the world while remaining fully aware of them. It is not a question of liking that which we do not like; it is a question of allowing it to exist and being willing to peacefully coexist with it. And then letting it go.

To practise loving-kindness does not mean to use sentiment. Just thinking about loving-kindness is not enough. Practising means enduring—allowing something unpleasant to be unpleasant, being alert to unpleasantness without allowing the mind to go into aversion. Now, how do we do that? We experiment with physical pain. When we have discomfort, we can have loving-kindness for it. We can allow pain to exist and we can actually peacefully coexist with it, not creating anything around it in our minds. We can concentrate on that pain and be with it, without an attitude of wanting to get rid of it. Some people have a big caveman's club with 'loving-kindness' written across it. They think: 'If I hit that pain with this loving-kindness, it'll go away.' But we should not use loving-kindness in that way to get rid of things; we should use it to remind ourselves to be extremely patient with all the unpleasantnesses of existence—the ugliness of life, the pain, the disappointments, the disillusionments, the failures.

When we do not create anything in it, the mind becomes clear. The mind itself, the original mind, the unconditioned, is clear, bright and peaceful, and can contain anything. We can allow all the rubbish in the universe to pass through this original mind and no harm will come to it. Nothing can soil or damage the original mind.

When we are not aware, we get caught in the way things seem to be. We think: 'I shouldn't be like that.' 'The world shouldn't be this way. I don't like it this way.' 'I don't want to be here; I want to be over there.' We become possessive, envious, jealous, averse, angry, hateful, greedy, lustful, frightened, miserly; we anticipate, dread and so forth, endlessly on and on. The chitchat, the rubbish that churns around, the bubbling inside—it will never end. We think: 'That's my real character;

my real character is just rubbish; I must be rubbish myself with all that rubbish in there.' But actually all that rubbish is just what we are not. When we are kindly, very gentle, very patient, not rushing, we shall realise that. We say: 'But I've got to do this, got to develop concentration, got to develop loving-kindness, got to develop all that and then I want to astral travel! So many things I've got to do. Be with pain and rubbish? I don't want to waste my life peacefully coexisting with rubbish! I want to get rid of rubbish—astral travel, do something worth while, achieve something, and attain! Can't be peaceful with this foul rubbish gurgling around inside.' When we react like this, when we have the idea of wanting to get rid of rubbish, we add more rubbish to the rubbish. The rubbish needs to come to consciousness; it is not going to go away on a clandestine path, disappear suddenly out of the back door; we have to allow it to come up into the mind and then out. When we establish the moral precepts and become really mindful, then the channel for this rubbish to flow through is very clear and safe. What we need to do is patiently endure and wisely reflect until the way out is clearly developed. With this attitude the conditions do not matter any more, good or bad.

Whether conditions are important, trivial, clean or dirty, they are all still conditions. We have no need to look through the rubbish inspecting it, because it is all just rubbish! We can let it go. Now, it takes equanimity not to get caught in conditions. We have given so much of our lives to doing just that, to being caught up, because we are, in fact, attached to the quality of conditions—choosing this, trying to get rid of that, a lifetime of picking and choosing, filtering, collecting, annihilating, hoarding, trying to hold onto, trying to possess.

Suppose we were to go to a river, look at a sand grain and say: 'Isn't that gorgeous! Isn't that a magnificent little sand grain. But isn't that one disgusting! I can't stand him.' All those sand grains, billions of them, and we are picking them out and liking or disliking each one according to its appearance, going into ecstasies over the beauty of one sand grain, or becoming depressed over the ugliness of another—ridiculous! If you saw someone doing that, you would think he was a real nut. And he would be depressed if he was holding on to an ugly sand grain! But most of us do that sort of thing, we do it with the conditions of the mind. We are elated or depressed by sand grains or conditions—they are much the same thing. When we see conditions as sand grains, we do not feel the need to compare one with another, or go into ecstasies or depressions over their appearance. So it is worth seeing conditions as sand grains. There is no need to dwell in aversion on the ugly, or become possessive and ecstatic over the beautiful. We can have equanimity, coolness, detachment and see conditions as just that—conditions.

To be mindful of the whole is a real possibility. All we have to do is free ourselves of constantly attaching to different conditions that come and go—grabbing this, rejecting that. How do we do this? We just become aware! At first the habitual tendency to grab is a real problem. So, when we find ourselves grabbing at something, we have to remind ourselves to leave it alone and let it be. After a while, our tendency to pick things up diminishes.

We can use words like 'letting go' to remind ourselves to put things down, leave them alone and not create problems around them. When we become attached to something and start worrying and suffering over it, that is the time to let it go. We should really investigate this attachment, observe what we are doing. We may, of course, be frightened of letting go because we do not know what will happen to us as a result. So we may have a lot of fear: 'If I let go of my desires and worries, there won't be anything left. Might dissolve! Might just disappear!' We have been carrying the burden for so long, we actually believe that the burden is us and so we cannot imagine life without it. The idea of letting the burden go is similar to the idea of killing ourselves. When we think about letting go of all our desires and fears, there is a feeling of annihilating ourselves. But once we do let go of the burden, we then know what it is like to not have problems! Then we are able to see clearly—minds alert to the moment, adaptable to time and place, no longer caught up in the momentum of habit and conditions.

So many people in the world, so much danger, so much misery! To learn from the rubbish of our minds is within our capability, but it does take determination and confidence. We may find ourselves sometimes on a plateau of dreariness, seemingly endless plains that go on, one after the other: 'Why did I ever start meditating?' 'Wish I had never thought of it.' But if we do not turn back, if we cross that plateau, that desert, enduring the monotony of our minds, then we shall know what it is like on the other side.

Being the Knowing

If I say 'yesterday' you remember something. And that is a perception conditioned into the mind. We carry all kinds of things around with us from the past, believing in them. How many of us give life to the past in the present? We have this ability to remember. When we are heedless, we do stupid things which we then have to remember. And we think: 'Maybe I should be more careful about what I do, so that when I remember, it won't be so dreadful.'

A young lady came to see me once who was really upset. She had had an abortion and was worried about the result of it, karmically. 'What will happen to me? When I die, what will happen then?' I said: 'I don't know. But you can observe the results here in this life. You have to remember these things, and wonder about them—that is the karmic result.'

When we do things like that, we have to remember them. And we have to wonder: 'Was it an evil thing to do? Was it all right? Should I have . . . shouldn't I?' We want to be told it is all right to do certain things, to have abortions. We want some kind of security. Or we want to have the living daylights scared out of us, and be told that what we have done is evil and wicked and we shall suffer in hell. But we do not know, do we? We do not know how wicked we are. Abortion is certainly not something one is going to advise people to have, unless there is some medical reason. One does not go around praising it as a noble, fine thing, holding it up and saying that it is the ultimate in attainment for a woman.

This is the kind of thing in life which always leaves the mind a little insecure or frightened— because we do not know. What we *can* know is that we do not know and that maybe we should live a little more carefully in the future so as not to have to make these kinds of decisions again, or have this kind of fear generated into our lives.

If we open the mind, wisely reflect, then we know how to live. There is no question of being told that we shall go to hell if we do this or that. People do go to hell, of course; they create it out of fear, doubt and anxiety—the results of living heedlessly. We remember the evil things we do; we do not forget those things, ever. We also remember the good things. But the point is, we have to remember. Indifferent things, ordinary things—we do not remember much of these. But anything extreme—a bit frightening or threatening—we do remember. This is the way the mind works.

The Buddha advised wise consideration—to wisely learn from life rather than just blindly living it as a creature of habit, or as a conditioned moral being. To be moral out of fear is better than being immoral, but still there is no wisdom in it.

So, the past is a memory NOW. But tomorrow? What is tomorrow? Tomorrow is the unknown, isn't it? How many things can happen tomorrow, in the unknown? We might think: 'Tomorrow I'll do this.' But things change and we may not be able to do this tomorrow. We can project into the future all possibilities from our experiences in the past:

'Maybe I will become a billionaire.' 'Maybe I will lose everything, have cancer, be deserted by everybody, have no friends left, live in some old slummy part of London—depressed and alone.' We can imagine the worst possible scenario, or the best, or anything in between. If it is suggested, say, that tomorrow will be the beginning of the Third World War, we may think: 'Oh, I dread that. Tomorrow! Oh, I hope tomorrow never comes.' Or someone might say: 'Tomorrow is going to be the Great Aquarian Age, the golden age for mankind where we'll actually grow up a bit and live like decent beings.' Then we might think: 'Oh, wouldn't that be wonderful! Tomorrow everything is going to be all right.' So, will there be a nuclear war tomorrow? Will it be the fulfilment of the Aquarian Age where everything will be wonderful?

What actually is waiting for us in the future? Death is waiting. We say: 'I don't want to think about that. I'll think about the past, look through my photograph album, look at videos of the wedding, the children getting their university degrees, me winning the golf tournament, me on a camel by the pyramids, me at the Vatican.' We are like that, aren't we? Why? Because the future is the unknown and rather than looking at that, we seek the past—memories, sentiment. In meditation we need to establish ourselves in the present—the known and the unknown.

The Buddhist teaching is that all that arises passes away and is not self. So death, what we call death, is nothing but the ending of a body. And yet this idea of dying is frightening to most of us because it is what we do not know: 'When I don't have this body any more, what will happen to me?' It is the unknown and we cannot imagine what will happen to us. Maybe we have perceptions about going to heaven, living happily ever after, living in a state of eternal bliss, joining the Father in heaven, playing a harp, radiating light. Or maybe going to hell: 'I'm just one of those people they send down to the pits.' We do not know the future. But we do not need to know. We can let the future be the mysterious unknown, the infinite potential—the possibility for pleasure, the possibility for pain, the possibility for peace. As we let go of the fear of the unknown, we find peace.

There is the 'now', and the 'knowing' that the past is a memory and the future is the unknown. This is the way to get the proper perspective on everything in the universe. We actually believe in time—yesterday and tomorrow—as solid realities. But they are just perceptions taking place in the present. We bring awareness to the way things are in the present. Each day can be taken as it comes, as a completely new experience, the perception of the date being seen as a convention for getting through time.

We know a lot *about* things from conditioned perceptions which we call education. We get our minds filled with a lot of ideas, facts, statistics—'The population of Britain is 55 million.' We think we really know something about Britain when we have that—'55 million people'. We say: 'Britain has 55 million people in it! That is an awful lot of people. It's overcrowded!' All this is just perception. We think we *really* know Britain because we know facts about it. But what is this knowledge actually? It is just a perception in the moment. That particular perception comes into consciousness, then it goes. We look upon 'Britain' as a reality, as solid, dependable, secure. Yet, when we *really* look at it, what is it? It is just a perception that comes and goes according to conditions. Unless we are obsessed, or crazy, we do not think 'Britain, Britain, Britain,' all the time. When certain conditions arise, then that particular perception comes into consciousness. And yet there is the proliferating tendency, the reactions if one is pro or anti, or has a lot of opinions and views: 'Britain—55 million people—overcrowded!' One thing goes on to the next. We say: 'America—Ronald Reagan—California.' There is an association of thought: 'Egypt—Pyramids—Cleopatra—Sadat.' When I was a child learning about China, we were told that Chinese women bound their feet. Even to this day, though Chinese women no longer bind their feet, that thought still comes up in my mind. So we can see how conditioned the mind is.

When meditating, we look at the habits of mind, the opinions, views and prejudices that we are conditioned with. We all have them. It is part of being human, part of human ignorance, to be caught in fixed positions about everything, about ourselves, religion, politics, all these things.

We can see them as perceptions in the mind. In meditation we recognise the limits of the mind. To do so is *being the knowing here and now.* Being the knowing—that which knows; knowing the limits of our human condition, of what we can know and what we cannot know; knowing what a memory is, what a concept is, or what a mental creation is—knowing conditions of the mind. The only certainty is right now—*this* is the way it is at this moment in time.

In the mornings I say: 'Today is the beginning of a new day. Yesterday is a memory. Tomorrow is the unknown. Now is the knowing.' This is a way to remember these things.

He Did Not Pass the Cakes

We get so busy, don't we? 'I just don't have time; I'm so busy, I don't have time to meditate.' We think that life is many important things to do. One time at Wat Pah Pong a Thai lady came from Bangkok to see Ajahn Chah and she said: 'I want to meditate but I just don't have time; I'm so busy.' He looked at her and said: 'Do you have time to eat?' She said: 'Well of course!' Eating is something we can always make time for; meditation we put off.

What is really important in our lives? What are the priorities? We have to decide what is more important, what it is that we really have to do. Worldly values are ones where the pull is to enjoy and participate in all that goes on; we think *that* is the real world. The spiritual world we may consider to be not so real. But everything that arises passes away and is not self—that is the Buddha's teaching. It is not a teaching to make us *believe* we do not have a self: 'I believe I don't exist, don't have any self.' It is not that. But body and mind just are not self. Schizophrenia is not self; depression is not self; anger is not self; paranoia is not self; fear is not self; desire is not self; greed is not self; jealousy is not self; the body is not self; being a man is not self; being a woman . . . the whole thing—not self.

Fear crosses our minds: 'I'm a terrible coward; that's the problem with me.' And we believe it! So we become cowardly. But if a cowardly thought goes through our minds and we say: 'Not self! That is not me,' it is like a fly crossing—there it goes! However, we tend to hold onto fear: 'That's me; that's what I really am. I'm that cowardly, weak, awful thing. That is what I really am.' And that is called 'self', 'ego'. But we do not want to be like that, so we think: 'Maybe I should be something else.' And we try to become what we would like to be.

We try to get praise; we try to get someone out

there to come and reinforce our worth. We learn to be charming, clever. People say: 'You're charming, clever and witty!' We say: 'That's me. Life's a party. I'm a delight to the world. I'm a gift to humanity.' So then we become conceited and arrogant. But that too is insecure. We have to keep getting the reinforcement all the time, and then we become a nuisance. People can only take so much of our charm and wit; it becomes boring after awhile. They say: 'Won't he ever stop?'

Or we may have an image of ourselves as being sensitive: 'I am a sensitive, spiritual being.' We can go around thinking that, reciting lovely little bits of poetry, talking about flowers. We all have these little games we play, these identities we try to act out in public, things we would like to be. What we actually are, of course, might be very different and beneath the facade, there is the fear of being dis-covered: 'I'm worthless, boring, nobody, nobody important; nobody could possibly love me.' We hope not to be found out. There is aspiration in our lives—wanting to become a noble being, somebody worthy of respect. But sometimes we do not know how to go about it. We may think that if we dazzle people with a few clever things and a charming appearance, that will do it. But it is all easily seen through.

In all human societies—tribal, civilised, or whatever—there is aspiration for the truth. Even in modern materialist societies, the aspiration is towards being very rational. We can look at all the injustices and things wrong with the present situation. We can think of how it should be, write it out and publish it—according to a rational ideal of how we would like the world to be. And when we read it, we think: 'Wouldn't it be wonderful if it were like that. It'd be great. That's the way it should be.' We can all agree on that; we have these ideals.

University life is filled with ideals. When I was a student in an American university, we spent a long time drinking beer and criticising everything—American government, American economy, American civilisation, American values; we knew how America *should* be. I could tell you how Britain should be. I could tell you how *you* should be. Do you want to hear? Then you can tell me how I should be. It is easy, isn't it? All of us are good at that. I can tell you how I think women should be—they should be kind, generous, loving, obedient, faithful, intelligent, hard-working, courageous, brave, noble-hearted, delicate, sweet, never a cross word, never a frown! That is how I would like all women to be, just for my sake. Men should be strong, brave, noble beings, hard-working, intelligent, enduring! I can tell everyone how they should be according to how I would like them to be for me, how I would like the British government to be, or the American government, the French, the Soviet.

No matter how much we want things to be otherwise, they are as they are. We know how we would like to sit in meditation, for example, as an ideal meditator. But how are we really? What goes on? Whatever it is, that is what we have to observe and learn from. Meditation is not a kind of analysis, putting a judgement on things, but a recognition of the way things are *at this moment*—not believing that things are like 'this' in a permanent way, but just recognising them as they are *in the moment*.

You think how you would like to be at home,

and how you would like everybody else to be at home. Your mind is quiet, and you want everybody else to be quiet. You go to work feeling very kind and calm, and you want everybody to respect that, not to say harsh things or stir you up, or make you angry. It takes a lot of energy, doesn't it, just trying to stop yourself from hitting somebody at the office! The world is an irritating, frustrating place; there is an incredible amount of friction in society, in families, in situations.

We can be irritated with each other even when sitting quietly in meditation! How many of us have felt really irritated by the habits of those around us—just wanting to bash them, wishing they would go away, leave? They might scratch themselves at a time when we do not want them to and we find that very annoying. Or they might move, or say something and we do not want to listen to it. So even in the most idyllic conditions we can get very irritated.

We need to take into account the conditions we have to exist with, not condemning or judging them, but just recognising them. These are the people; they are 'this' way—the people at the office, in the factory, in the hospital, at home. This is what we have to exist with, be patient with, reflect on, these kinds of people, these kinds of situations. 'I don't want it like this. I hate it!' With this attitude we make a suffering situation for ourselves. But we can reflect and allow the friction that arises in the mind to become a fully conscious experience—just frustration, or anger, or resentment. Then we know what it is and do not push it aside, trying to repress it, or we do not indulge in it. We may go to the office on Monday morning and somebody says something very irritating: 'I'm going to leave! I'm going to quit this! I'm . . . I'm not going to put up with this any more!' We get carried away. Alternatively, we can just watch, reflect on the feeling that arises in the mind, the irritation. What is that irritation? We can observe it, have the time, the patience, to just observe the feeling that arises from friction.

Sitting in meditation is the same; after a time—physical pain! We should observe that pain rather than try to get rid of it. An itch: 'I hate that itch! I want to scratch it.' Then: 'But I shouldn't scratch it.' After that we get caught in wanting to scratch, then wanting *not* to scratch. What do we do? Scratch? Not scratch? We can make a real problem out of it. Or we can go right to the sensation itself, go right to the itching—with the mind, that is, not with the hand. We can concentrate right on that itching feeling, that unpleasant sensation that we want to get rid of, and just be patient with it. This state of: 'Maybe I should scratch? No, no, I should just be patient with it,' that is suffering, isn't it? But actually going right to the sensation itself, concentrating on it, is quite bearable, it is all right.

The same applies to irritations in our minds. We go to the office. Somebody has done something all wrong; he is being really stupid. We want to blow up. Now, we can go right to that feeling of anger or frustration; as with the itch, we can concentrate on it, right in the heart, listen to it, make it a fully conscious thing—and then let it go. It goes away. And we have not been foolish, we have not said anything, done anything that we would later regret. We can easily get caught up in depression or the desire to run away. But we should take into account that the world is like this. There is always going to be plenty of friction, irritation, wherever we go. There is plenty in the monastery, and there is plenty in family life—even in happy marriages.

The sensory world is one of irritation and friction. But if we use it, we shall become very patient, gentle, mellow creatures, lovely, wise beings. Anyone who practises with that friction wisely becomes gentle and soft. The friction grinds away all the hard edges, the nastiness and harshness of our minds.

There was a monk I knew once. He kept all the cakes for himself! I was sitting in the line of monks at the meal with my little bowl of sticky rice and bamboo shoots, waiting for some cakes to be passed down. Talk about friction in the mind! I looked up after awhile and saw that monk at the head of the line with a mischievous gleam in his eye—he was not going to send those cakes down. I observed the desire to murder—the frustration, the wanting, the resentment at someone stopping me having something I thought I deserved: 'Those cakes were given for *all* the monks; they weren't given for just that *one* monk. That is a dirty trick to play on the lay people. Those generous kind

lay people came; they brought those cakes, and they want to see us *all* eating them, not just *him!'* I really got indignant, righteously indignant, because I was right: 'If those people had brought cakes for just that one monk, they would not have brought so many.' I sat there fuming; and I had indigestion for the rest of the day—all because I lacked the ability to concentrate on friction. Actually in the long run it has made a very good story.

The point is, I did not die; nobody was deprived of nourishment that day. We all survived. These things are really silly things in our lives. And we can get very upset even to the point of murder over some foolish little thing. I was amazed to find how easy it was to get so overwhelmed with anger over such a trivial matter.

In daily-life meditation we use the difficult situations—the irritations, the unsatisfactoriness, the dreariness, the disappointments, all that is negative and unpleasant about life—for wise reflection. It is an opportunity to concentrate, to develop. We can turn to the sensation itself, rather than trying to straighten out the world by telling it how it should be.

'You know that monk? Well, he shouldn't be that way. That isn't the right way for a good monk. A good monk should share everything—in fact, maybe give up his share for someone else. A good monk shouldn't be one that keeps everything for himself and doesn't pass down the cakes! 'We can all agree on what a good monk should be. 'Is a good monk one who hoards up food for himself? No! Is a good monk one who looks after himself at the expense of everyone else? No! Is a good monk one who doesn't care about himself, just takes what he needs and shares the rest? Yes! That is a good monk!' So I could go and tell that monk what he should be. But he already knows! He knows what he should be. He knew at the time, and he knew what I was thinking—that was obvious from the glint in his eye. All there is left for me to do is go to the sensation, the anger, the heat, where it really hurts—here, inside. That kind of practice makes us very soft; we become very, very patient.

Thai monasteries are not terribly efficient; that, of course, is not their purpose. And for years Ajahn Chah would not allow electricity. The wealthy people came and wanted to put electric pumps on the wells to make it easier for us, but Ajahn Chah declined the offer. And he made sure we went out every day with ropes, pulleys and buckets to draw the water, carry it on poles, and distribute it to containers in the kitchen and to the bathing areas. Primitive, wasn't it? And very inefficient. But it demanded a lot of patience, a willingness to do routine things—day after day after day—until eventually we found them to be quite peaceful activities. 'It is certainly primitive out here. No mains water, no electricity. It's backward, inefficient!' I could think of how it *should* be, but that was not the point. The patience, the willingness to endure, the willingness to do routine things over and over again, the willingness to endure the mosquitoes and all the other things—that was the point. The weather is hot, the mosquitoes are biting, I am sitting in meditation: 'I'm going to get malaria! I know it!' Maybe six or seven of them are biting at once. Horrible feeling. Aversion arises, incredible anger and frustration. What is there to do? The only thing worth doing is going to the aversion itself, to the sensation, and investigating it. That was how I began to endure what was seemingly unendurable. And I found that kind of practice to be very helpful. I did not like it at the time, of course, but it was very beneficial.

Frustrations, difficulties in our daily lives—we can use them for meditation. We can just keep facing the things that come up in our minds, the fears and desires. And we become someone who reflects and learns from life, not someone who always complains and feels disappointed when life fails to come up to expectations. Being able to work with life as it is, with ourselves, with the people we live with, with the society we live in—that is meditation in daily life.

We have the opportunity to become enlightened beings. We can concentrate, observe, understand, really know what desire is, know what fear is, know what is present, know that whatever is present is an impermanent condition, and know that impermanent conditions are not self. We can keep penetrating our fears and desires, and then we shall no longer be deluded by them.

It takes constant practice, of course, because most of us operate from conditioning. We have a way of living at home, at the office, or wherever, out of habit, and have become used to living and acting in certain ways. We have found security and safety in that routine, in things we feel we can depend on. But that very sense of security and safety is dangerous! The things that we think are safe really are not; they can be changed, disrupted or taken away from us at any time. Then we feel distraught, resentful, upset. What can we do? We can go to the source, go right to where it is, where we can witness it, know it, concentrate on it, really see it as it is. And then, if we no longer blindly follow our feelings of the moment, we shall begin to realise the peace of our minds. We can turn to that peacefulness, the unconditioned, the continuous silence of the mind; we can just turn to that instead of to the sensation. An itch now comes; we turn to the silence rather than to the sensation. If we try to turn to the silence out of aversion for the sensation, however, it will not work. We have to be scrupulously honest and patient. At first we have to turn to the sensation, be fully with it, patiently, being willing to endure, allowing it to be as it is, allowing it to be our meditation until it stops.

Even in the midst of agony, despair, or restlessness, we can get to the source of it, rather than running away from it. Then, when we know these things beyond doubt, we just go to the silence of the mind.

If we are really willing to allow that which is most upsetting to be there, or that which is most boring, or most frightening, concentrating on it, welcoming it even, then we shall be taking an opportunity to be patient, gentle, wise. And this is the way to develop the path in our lives as human beings from now until the death of our bodies. I look back over my life as a monk. I really resented some of the most difficult situations at the time, but now I view them with affection; I realise now that they were strengthening experiences. At the time I thought: 'I wish this wasn't happening, I wish I could get rid of this.' But now I look back with enormous gratitude because they were beneficial experiences.

Anguish, despair, sorrow can be transmuted into patient endurance, into wise reflection. Life is as it is. Some of it is going to be very nice, some of it awful. A lot of it is going to be neither nice nor awful, just boring. Life is like that. We observe: 'This is how our lives have to be.' Then we wisely use what we have, learn from it, and free ourselves from the narrow limits of self and mortality.

Other Publications from

Buddhist
   Publishing
      Group

The Old Zen Master:
Inspirations for Awakening.
Trevor Leggett
Teaching stories and encounters
from Zen and other religions.
2000, 147pp.

An Introduction to Buddhism
Advice on treading the Buddhist
path, with easy-to-follow instruc-
tions.
Diana St Ruth
1988, 92pp.

Zen Teaching of Instantaneous
Awakening
Hui Hai (also known as Pai-chang
Huai Hai). Trans. **John Blofeld**
A classic eighth-century Zen text.
1987/95, 144pp.

Experience Beyond Thinking
A practical guide to Buddhist
meditation.
Diana St Ruth
1993, 127pp.

Zen Graffiti
Insightful verses in the Zen style.
Azuki
1991, 94pp.

Mud and Water
A collection of talks by **Zen
Master Bassui** (C14 Japan).
Trans. **Arthur Braverman**
1989, 128pp

Printed in the United Kingdom
by Lightning Source UK Ltd.
108892UKS00001B/181